"As the Small Rain"

by

BOB JONES, JR., Litt.D., L.H.D., LL.D.
Acting President, Bob Jones College
Cleveland, Tennessee

THIRD EDITION

ZONDERVAN PUBLISHING HOUSE
Grand Rapids, Michigan

My doctrine shall drop as the rain, my speech shall distil as the dew, as the small rain upon the tender herb, and as the showers upon the grass.
Deuteronomy 32:2

PUBLISHER'S FOREWORD

These articles, under the title "A Look at the Book," originally appeared in a syndicated column published in several hundred newspapers. It is conservatively estimated that in this form they have been read by several million people.

From a great many of the columns appearing over a period of years the publishers have selected those included in this volume. Not only do they afford rich spiritual reading, but they also provide outlines, material and ideas for the construction of sermons and devotional messages. An appropriate poem in harmony with the theme of each article has been included. Together they offer interesting material for a brief radio broadcast.

CONTENTS

"The Entrance of Thy Words Giveth Light"

"Now Is the Day of Salvation"

"I Am the Door"

"Because I Live, Ye Shall Live Also"

Contents

Contents

"Be Not Afraid, But Speak"

"What Shall I Render Unto the Lord?"

"The Entrance of Thy Words Giveth Light"
Psalm 119:130

NO OTHER NAME

"THE devil can cite Scripture for his purpose." Shakespeare puts these words into the mouth of one of his characters in *The Merchant of Venice,* and the Scriptures themselves bear evidence of the accuracy of Shakespeare's observation, for the devil in tempting Christ quoted the Word of God. Evil and dishonest men have never hesitated to use a passage of Scripture in an attempt to justify their wrong course of action or to excuse their evil-doing. Of course, such a procedure is in itself evil and dishonest since the Scripture is by them misquoted or misused or misapplied. The Word of God nowhere admonishes men to a course of action which violates the law of God.

Whatever else the Scriptures may or may not prove, they do testify that the Lord Jesus Christ is God manifest in the flesh. It is a sad fact that by many people today this great and primary truth of the Book is overlooked or forgotten.

Apollos preaching at Ephesus convinced his hearers, "shewing by the Scriptures that Jesus was Christ" (Acts 18:28). Christ Himself admonished His hearers to "search the Scriptures; for in them ye think ye have eternal life; and they are they which testify of me" (John 5:39). Christ is the center of the Book, the burden of the prophet's message, the theme of the psalmist's lay, the chief character of the Gospels, the fountainhead and inspiration of the Epistles, the sublime and majestic central figure of Revelation.

The Bible discloses God's purpose and love for man. It is God's Written Word. Christ is the Incarnate Word—the Word of God come in the flesh. The Bible speaks of Christ. Christ manifests in His own wonderful Person the truth of the Bible.

9

Men today wrest the Scriptures to prove their own pet theories and opinions. They are glibly quoting Scripture without regard for its purpose or true teaching. But the man who searches the Word diligently with an open mind cannot fail to be convinced of the fact that Jesus is the Christ, the One come in the flesh to redeem men from sin by the blood which He shed upon Calvary's cross. He must admit the truth of the Bible's teaching that "there is none other name under heaven given among men, whereby we must be saved." In the sacred pages of Holy Writ, God the Father claims Christ as His Son, proclaims His deity, acclaims His perfections. Through the Word the Father speaks to us of the Christ, "This is my beloved Son: hear him."

O Word of God Incarnate,
O Wisdom from on high,
O Truth unchanged, unchanging,
O Light of our dark sky;
We praise Thee for the radiance
That from the hallowed page,
A lantern to our footsteps,
Shines on from age to age.

The Church from her dear Master
Received the gift divine,
And still that light she lifteth
O'er all the earth to shine.
It is the golden casket
Where gems of truth are stored;
It is the heav'n-drawn picture
Of Christ the living Word.

It floateth like a banner
Before God's host unfurled;
It shineth like a beacon
Above the darkling world;
It is the chart and compass
That o'er life's surging sea,
'Mid mists and rocks and quicksands
Still guides, O Christ, to Thee.

—*William W. How*

THE CRITICS FAIL

I HAVE watched a scientist, as he lectured on the wonders of botany, tear a flower petal from petal and part from part until there was no flower left. That which had been beautiful was destroyed. Instead of the perfect loveliness of the blossom there were scattered petals and yellow pollen. In his efforts to discover for himself or point out to others the intricate structure of the flower, he destroyed it. Vivisectionists have cut up living bodies trying to discover the secret of life and in the process they have destroyed life.

The so-called "higher critics" remind one of the botanist and the vivisectionist. They seek to tear apart the Word of God. Verse by verse, chapter by chapter, book by book, author by author, they untwist and unwind and pry apart. They dissect that which is a living whole.

Of course, man cannot destroy the Bible. God's Word is forever fixed in heaven. Higher criticism, which never takes into account the inspiration of the Holy Spirit and the supernatural character of the Scripture, can never destroy the Word which is as eternal as the God who gave it. In their effort to prove their own theories as to authorship and to discover contradictions in the Word where no contradictions exist, they only dull further the blunt blades of their own intellectual instruments.

The sad part about the whole process, however, is this. As far as their own perception is concerned they miss the beauty of the flower which they seek to analyze and divide part from part. Though they can never destroy the living Word, they are unconscious that it is living and vital and as they cut out a fragment here and a fragment there, they fail to find the eternal life which God's Word offers to them, for this book from Genesis to Revelation speaks of Him who is the Life of God, the One who is the Author of eternal life, the One who came that man might have life. The Word of God is a whole. To the believer each portion is precious and each promise is sweet. The analysis of all the higher critics in the world cannot explain it. The wisdom of man cannot reproduce it any more than the botanist can make a flower or the scientist give life.

> Last eve I paused beside the blacksmith's door,
>   And heard the anvil ring the vesper chime;
> Then looking in, I saw upon the floor,
>   Old hammers worn with beating years of time.
>
> "How many anvils have you had," said I,
>   "To wear and batter all these hammers so?"
> "Just one," said he, and then, with twinkling eye,
>   "The anvil wears the hammers out, you know."
>
> "And so," I thought, "The Anvil of God's Word
>   For ages sceptic blows have beat upon,
> Yet, though the noise of falling blows was heard,
>   The Anvil is unharmed, the hammers gone."
>
> —*John Clifford*

* * *

FOOLISH PREACHING

PEOPLE have a way of saying, "I would read the Bible more except that I cannot understand it." Many Bible scholars will agree that there are certain parts in the Book whose meaning they cannot understand. This is no reflection on the Bible, however, but rather upon the low spiritual understanding of man. I doubt if there are any two students of the Bible who will agree completely on the interpretation of every part of the Word, but the Bible is always clear and explicit and easily understood when it tells a man what he needs to know in order to be saved. "Believe on the Lord Jesus Christ, and thou shalt be saved."

"There is none other name under heaven given among men, whereby we must be saved," says Peter speaking of Christ. The Son of God Himself made the way of salvation perfectly plain when He said, "I am the way, the truth, and the life: no man cometh unto the Father, but by me." In those words, called the heart of the Gospel (John 3:16), the way of salvation is again plainly stated: "For God so loved the world, that he gave his only begotten Son, that whosoever believeth in him should not perish, but have everlasting life." It is not understanding the Bible that saves man. It is trusting Christ.

Some men have not read enough of the Bible to know whether they understand it or not, but this much is certain: when you have trusted Christ as your Saviour, and love Him, you will find a love for the Bible and a desire to read it. The one who reads the Bible with faith in the Christ whom the Book reveals, finds that much which was, before his conversion, beyond his comprehension, now has become clear and plain.

In his first letter to the Corinthian Church, Paul says, "The preaching of the cross is to them that perish foolishness." That is, the Gospel of the grace of God seems a foolish thing to those who have not experienced it. He continues, "But unto us which are saved it is the power of God." As a child of God, having experienced His grace, one understands the Word of God in a way in which the unsaved never can. The Book itself is explicit on this point: "But the natural man receiveth not the things of the Spirit of God: for they are foolishness unto him: neither can he know them, because they are spiritually discerned." The man who is born of the Spirit, who has had a personal experience with God, will understand many things in the Word of God which were beyond his comprehension before he was saved. But anyone can interpret the plain meaning of Scripture where the Book points the way of salvation.

> The Spirit breathes upon the Word,
>   And brings the truth to sight;
> Precepts and promises afford
>   A sanctifying light.

A glory gilds the sacred page
Majestic like the sun;
It gives a light to every age—
It gives, but borrows none.

—William Cowper

*   *   *

FOR ALL MEN

A MISSIONARY traveling in the Near East stopped for the night in the tent of a shepherd whom he had visited several years before. The old nomad greeted him with the question, "Did you bring back the sheep book?" For a moment the missionary was at a loss to understand the meaning of the question. Then it occurred to him that when he had last seen the old shepherd he had read to him in his own language the Twenty-third Psalm, and to this ignorant keeper of flocks the Bible was the "sheep book." He understood its language as it spoke about the Shepherd and the sheep. They were things with which he was familiar.

Wonderful Book! Each man finds in its pages something which seems addressed especially to him. The sinner sees his picture, painted by the hand of God in the words of the holy men of old, who "spake as they were moved by the Holy Ghost" (II Peter 1:21). He sees his sin set forth in all its blackness. Beholding himself pictured as God sees him, he becomes conscious of his need for a Saviour, and in the pages of the Bible the Saviour is presented, Jesus Christ who bore the guilt of the sinner on the cross and became the propitiation for his sin.

Lonely hearts find comfort as they turn its pages. The seekers after knowledge find divine truth. The Bible must be God's Book, for its appeal is broader than any nation or century or language or class of men. It sounds the depths of the human soul. It probes into the thoughts of the mind and the impulses instinctive in the human heart. Chinese hearing God's Word for the first time cry, "This Book was written for the Chinese." The women of India say it was written for them. Both are right. To them and to all men everywhere God speaks through the Bible, His own infallible Word.

> God, in the Gospel of His Son,
> Makes His eternal counsels known;
> Where love in all its glory shines,
> And truth is drawn in fairest lines.
>
> Here sinners of a humble frame
> May taste His grace, and learn His Name;
> May read, in characters of blood,
> The wisdom, pow'r and grace of God.
>
> The pris'ner here may break his chains;
> The weary rest from all his pains;
> The captive feel his bondage cease;
> The mourner find the way of peace.
>
> Here faith reveals to mortal eyes
> A brighter world beyond the skies;
> Here shines the light which guides our way
> From earth to realms of endless day.
>
> O grant us grace, Almighty Lord,
> To read and mark Thy holy Word;
> Its truths with meekness to receive,
> And by its holy precepts live.
>   —*Thomas Cotterill*

* * *

THE DIVINE AUTHOR

THE proof of the inspiration of Scripture may be found not only in that which the Bible contains, but also in that which is omitted from the Book. Were the Bible, like other books, only the product of the minds and hearts and experiences of human writers, there would have been many more details set down. The human instinct of curiosity about people and places and events would have been by human authors more fully satisfied. The record would have been embellished and colored and dramatized.

Take, for example, the Gospels. They contain the account of the life of our Lord upon earth. The four books together would make a very small volume, not more than can be read quite easily in a few hours' time. They deal with the greatest personality ever to appear on the stage of history. They are the record of His life, His ministry, His dramatic and tragic death, the stupendous miracle of His resurrection. Modern biographers write hundreds of pages about relatively unimportant men and women, but God, the Holy Spirit, through the instrumentality of Matthew, Mark, Luke and John, gives us this short account of the life among men of the Saviour of the world. Many of His deeds, much that He said, is left unrecorded. John himself toward the close of His book notes this, "And many other signs truly did Jesus in the presence of his disciples, which are not written in this book" (John 20:30). And, in the last verse, he gives us the reason for the things which the record does contain. "But these are written, that ye might believe that Jesus is the Christ, the Son of God; and that believing ye might have life through his name."

All that men need to know in order to be saved is found in the Word of God. God's dealings with men are there set forth. The Book records His law and declares His will. In reading it the sinner is convicted, the backslider admonished, the saint comforted. It not only points the way to heaven. It affords light and strength and joy to those who walk that Way.

> The heav'ns declare Thy glory, Lord,
> In ev'ry star Thy wisdom shines;
> But when our eyes behold Thy Word,
> We read Thy Name in fairer lines.

The rolling sun, the changing light,
And nights and days, Thy pow'r confess;
But the blest volume Thou didst write,
Reveals Thy justice and Thy grace.

Sun, moon, and stars convey Thy praise
Round the whole earth, and never stand;
So, when Thy truth began its race,
It touch'd and glanc'd on ev'ry land.

Nor shall Thy spreading Gospel rest,
Till thro' the world Thy truth has run;
Till Christ has all the nations blest
That see the light or feel the sun.

Great Sun of Righteousness, arise;
Bless the dark world with heavenly light;
The Gospel makes the simple wise;
Thy laws are pure, Thy judgments right.

Thy noblest wonders here we view,
In souls renewed, and sins forgiven;
Lord, cleanse our sins, our souls renew,
And make Thy Word our guide to heaven.

—*Isaac Watts*

*   *   *

BEST SELLER

THE Bible judged from any standpoint is an unusual and remarkable Book. The book of Job, the oldest portion according to the opinion of sound scholarship, is more than three thousand years old. The newest portion, the book of Revelation, was written about 96 A.D. Between these two books, through the intervening centuries, the others were written by approximately forty men. Yet there is not a single contradiction or discrepancy in the whole book.

The Bible is not a treatise on science, but when it deals with science it is scientifically accurate. It is not primarily a book of history, yet the archaeologist digging up the records of ancient civilization has proved over and over again its historical inerrancy. From every viewpoint it is the world's most valuable volume. Someone has said that wicked men would not have written the Bible because it reproves human wickedness. Good men would not have written it because it claims divine authorship.

The only explanation of the Book is found in the fact that the Bible "came not in old time by the will of man: but holy men of God spake as they were moved by the Holy Ghost" (II Peter 1:21). God Himself, through the instrumentality of His servants, who wrote under the inspiration of the Holy Spirit, is the Author of the Book.

The Word has a radiant and transforming power over mind and heart and life. "The entrance of thy words giveth light" (Psalm 119:130). The Word of God throws light upon the relationship of man with man, nation with nation, and upon the relationship of men and nations with God. There is no other volume which so stimulates the mind and enlightens the intellect.

But the Bible does more than bring intellectual enlightenment. It expels spiritual darkness in the human heart and brings the light of the very presence of God Himself into the souls of those who accept its promises and trust the Redeemer whom it reveals. The man who believes and loves the Book finds it a lamp to his feet in the darkness of this world and a light on the path which he walks (Psalm 119: 105). The Book gives light. The Book is light. The Word of God treasured in the human heart dispels the darkness of sin. The psalmist has written, "Thy word have I hid in mine heart, that I might not sin against thee" (Psalm 119: 11). The Word inwardly pondered affects outward action. The Word of God hidden in the human heart does not stay hidden. Like a bright flame in a lamp, its light shines out through the life.

Though the cover is worn
And the pages are torn,
And though places bear traces of tears,
  Yet more precious than gold
  Is the Book, worn and old,
That can shatter and scatter my fears.

When I prayerfully look
In the precious old Book,
Many pleasures and treasures I see;
  Many tokens of love
  From the Father above,
Who is nearest and dearest to me.

This old Book is my guide,
'Tis a friend by my side,
It will lighten and brighten my way;
  And each promise I find
  Soothes and gladdens my mind
As I read it and heed it today.

—*Anonymous*

*   *   *

"Now Is the Day of Salvation"

II Corinthians 6:2

NO FREEDOM IN FLATTERY

THERE is one sin greatly condemned in the Bible against which you almost never hear anyone preach. It is the sin of flattery, and how largely it is practiced these days. Some flatter with no malicious intent. They desire popularity and want people to like them, and so they cultivate the habit of saying that which will please the hearer without regard to its truth; or, they have read some popular book on psychology, which tells them that the way to make friends is to flatter, and they put into practice this advice with never a thought that they are being dishonest.

Others flatter for more malicious reasons. Politicians have discovered that the surest way to cause an opponent to make a fool of himself is to flatter him into doing something which in an uninflated state of mind he would have better judgment than to attempt. Others indulge in flattery to get something from the object of their flattery. They are like the fox in the fable who flattered the crow by praising his beautiful voice. When the crow, full of vanity, opened his beak to sing, he dropped the piece of cheese he was holding, and the fox gobbled it up.

Some people flatter from sheer cowardice. They lack the courage to speak the truth. They will say what another expects of them rather than what they know to be so. There are preachers who are guilty here. Instead of preaching against the sins of unregenerate human hearts, they flatter their hearers with smooth-sounding messages on the greatness of the human race. Sinners lost and undone feel no conviction as they sit under their ministry, but go out full of self-satisfaction to continue in their sin. They are trapped and pinioned in a net of smooth words, when if they had been told the truth about themselves and their own sinful condition and pointed to the Lord Jesus, they would have found in truth and in Him who is Truth, freedom from the chains of sin. Truly, "a man that flattereth his neighbour spreadeth a net for his feet" (Proverbs 29:5). There is no flattering of the Adamic nature and of sinners in God's Word. Unregenerate men hate and despise the Word of God because it tells them the truth about themselves. Men do not want the truth. Men prefer flattery, but it is only in the truth that freedom is found.

> Let not the wise their wisdom boast,
>   The mighty glory in their might,
> The rich in flattering riches trust,
>   Which take their everlasting flight.
>
> The rush of numerous years bears down
>   The most gigantic strength of man;
> And where is all his wisdom gone,
>   When dust he turns to dust again?
>
> One only gift can justify
>   The boasting soul that knows his God;
> When Jesus doth His blood apply,
>   I glory in His sprinkled blood.
>
> The Lord, my righteousness, I praise,
>   I triumph in the love divine,
> The wisdom, wealth and strength of grace,
>   In Christ to endless ages mine.
>
>   —*Charles Wesley*

* * *

PAGAN AMERICA

America is not a Christian country. There are Christians in America. Christian influences went into the building of our nation and the impact of Christian truth is still felt to some extent in our national law and life, but America is essentially and predominantly pagan.

The great majority of our people worship the same gods which were reverenced in ancient Greece and Rome. Of course, they are not called by their classical names nor recognized as deities, but they are worshiped none-the-less, though graven images are not set up and statues and altars are not erected to them.

When the ancients worshiped Jupiter or Mars or Venus, they were bowing down before some attribute or characteristic of their own human nature which they had deified. Athena was the deification of wisdom, Mars of war, Venus of lust. The deities were made in the image of their worshipers.

Today in America, though men do not burn incense on the altars dedicated to deities who are projections of their own characteristics and impulses and passions, they worship and serve these attributes and passions, for the thing which becomes supreme in their lives becomes the god of their lives.

There are some men who worship their own intellects. Their minds are their gods; wisdom is their chief pursuit. The standard by which they measure values is the standard of their own reasoning. Others sacrifice everything to greed; avarice is their god. They are devotees of wealth. Others are mastered by their appetite for drink. No priest of Bacchus was ever more zealous than they. Many live to serve the lust of the flesh and worship the base passions of their nature.

America is a pagan nation. America is not a Christian nation. It never will be until Christ becomes the Lord of our people.

> Dread Jehovah! God of nations!
> From Thy temple in the skies,
> Hear Thy people's supplications;
> Now for their deliverance rise.
>
> Lo! with deep contrition turning,
> In Thy holy place we bend;
> Hear us, fasting, praying, mourning;
> Hear us, spare us, and defend.

Though our sins, our hearts confounding,
  Long and loud for vengeance call,
Thou hast mercy more abounding;
  Jesus' blood can cleanse them all.

Let that mercy veil transgression;
  Let that blood our guilt efface:
Save Thy people from oppression;
  Save from spoil Thy holy place.

—Thomas Cotterill

* * *

MEN OF GOOD WILL

ABOUT two thousand years ago, Christ was born. Ever since men have sought the benefits which have come to earth as a result of His presence among the sons of men. At the same time, they have rejected Him.

How much blessing has come as a result of His life and teaching! Had He not been born, there would be no hospitals, no old people's homes, no orphanages, no asylums. Mercy, education, charity, equity—these always follow the preaching of the Gospel. Children have a debt to the Babe in the manger for the lot of children is happier where His Name is known. Motherhood received its crown from the One who on the cross said to John, "Behold thy mother" (John 19:27). Where the Christian religion is taught, woman is lifted from the slavery which she occupies under pagan teaching.

Man has welcomed all these benefits, but many have rejected Him from whom they come and turned their backs upon Him of whose way of life they are the fruit. They have sought the truth and rejected the Teacher of the truth. They have welcomed mercy but rejected God's Son who came to earth as the Gift of divine mercy. Is it any wonder that almost two thousand years after His birth the world is still torn asunder by war and aflame with strife! How can there be peace when the hearts of men are turned against the Prince of Peace? When He sojourned among men, God's Son "came unto his own, and his own received him not" (John 1:11), and down the ages ever since the world which He made has rejected Him. But always there has been a little group whose hearts were open to Him. It is to these few in every age and generation that peace has come. They are the "men of good will" in whose hearts the Prince of Peace has been enthroned. There He reigns, giving peace in the midst of all the conflict of nations and clash of opinions and the vain strife of man.

Since Jesus is my Friend,
And I to Him belong,
It matters not what foes intend,
However fierce and strong.

He whispers in my breast
Sweet words of holy cheer:
How they who seek in God their rest
Shall ever find Him near.

How God hath built above,
A city fair and new,
Where eye and heart shall see and prove
What faith has counted true.

My heart for gladness springs,
It cannot more be sad;
For very joy it laughs and sings—
Sees nought but sunshine glad.

The Sun that lights mine eyes
Is Christ, the Lord I love;
I sing for joy for that which lies
Stored up for me above.

—*Paul Gerhardt*

*   *   *

MORAL COWARDICE

Pontius Pilate was not a vicious man. He was a coward. He lacked the courage of his convictions. He lacked the strength of character to defy public opinion. He was afraid to risk his political position by doing what he knew was right.

As a judge he found Christ innocent of the charges brought against Him. He said, "I find no fault in this man" (Luke 23:4). Law and conscience demanded that He be released, but the leaders of Israel were determined to have His blood and "Pilate gave sentence that it should be as they required" (Luke 23:24). Pilate preferred to see this "just man" slain rather than risk the enmity of the Jewish leaders. He was afraid of what they might say to Caesar and feared that their lies might cost him his position as governor of Judea.

There are still plenty of Pilates in politics and in every other business of life as well. They would like to do what they know to be right, but they are afraid to take a position contrary to popular opinion. They think more of their own popularity than they do of justice. There are parents who permit their children to do things which are against their own conscience because other young people are doing those things, and because the parents lack the courage to be firm with their own children. There are teachers who compromise their convictions rather than offend some members of the school board. There are preachers who fail to preach against sin because they are afraid of stepping on the toe of some prominent member of the church.

We need nothing so much as firm conviction and the courage to stand by it. According to tradition, Pilate lost his position as governor of Judea after the crucifixion of Christ. He was recalled to Rome and sent into exile, where he died. Sacrificing his convictions, he sacrificed the respect of all men who know from the Bible the story of his cowardice. The man who compromises always loses the respect of those whose love and favor he seeks to gain.

In the hour of trial,
Jesus, plead for me;
Lest by base denial,
I depart from Thee.
When Thou seest me waver,
With a look recall,
Nor for fear or favor
Suffer me to fall.

With forbidden pleasures
Would this vain world charm,
Or its sordid treasures
Spread to work me harm,
Bring to my remembrance
Sad Gethsemane,
Or, in darker semblance,
Cross-crowned Calvary.

Should Thy mercy send me
Sorrow, toil and woe;
Or should pain attend me
On my path below,
Grant that I may never
Fail Thy hand to see,
Grant that I may ever
Cast my care on Thee.

—*James Montgomery*

* * *

PORK OR PARADISE

CHRIST came to the country of the Gadarenes, and they asked Him to depart from their coast. Why?

There was a poor outcast possessed of many demons living in the tombs of the hillside. From this fierce, unhappy creature the Lord Jesus Christ cast out the tormenting spirits, permitting them to go into a herd of swine. Unwilling to give habitation to the spirits that had controlled the man, the swine ran into the sea and were drowned (Mark 5:1-17).

These Gadarenes had the wrong sense of value. They

thought more of their pigs than they did of a man. They asked the Son of God to leave them because they preferred to see a man in the grip of demons rather than to lose some swine.

Some people are like that today. They think more of temporal gain than they do of eternal values. Some men are so busy attending to business that they have no time for their families, and in struggling to accumulate a fortune they let their own children go to destruction.

There are many people who refuse to let the Lord Jesus Christ come into their lives because they want to hold on to some selfish ambition or evil habit or sinful practice. They reject the Saviour because they do not want to give up some fleeting pleasure or worldly idol. They would rather have a few pigs than the presence of the Son of God and all the joy which His salvation brings. They would rather have hogs than heaven, pork than paradise. Christ says, "I am come that they might have life, and that they might have it more abundantly," but the Gadarenes among us prefer to keep their pigs. Indeed, there is a strange kinship between such men and their swine—both are satisfied with the gratification of the senses and both lack appreciation of intangible realities. The Lord Jesus Christ comes with an emphasis on the things of the Spirit—the unseen, permanent things. "What shall it profit a man," says Jesus, "if he shall gain the whole world, and lose his own soul?"

> Happy are they, they that love God,
> Whose hearts have Christ confessed,
> Who by His cross have found their life,
> And 'neath His yoke their rest.
>
> Glad is the praise, sweet are the songs,
> When they together sing;
> And strong the prayers that bow the ear
> Of Heaven's eternal King.

Christ to their homes giveth His peace,
And makes their loves His own;
But, ah, what tares the evil one
Hath in His garden sown!

Sad were our lot, evil this earth,
Did not its sorrows prove
The path whereby the sheep may find
The fold of Jesus' love.

Then shall they know, they that love Him,
How all their pain is good;
And death itself cannot unbind
Their happy brotherhood.

—Charles Coffin

* * *

DISTORTED PERSPECTIVE

ALL too often our perspective is wrong, our sense of values
is distorted. We are so occupied with perishable things. We
spend precious time on houses and clothes and food and
physical comforts. Clothes wear out, and houses fall down,
and food is consumed and forgotten. The body which we
care for and adorn and make comfortable, dies and goes back
to dust. We neglect our souls. They go unfed and uncared
for. We are not concerned about them. Yet, they are the
only part of us which lives forever.

The Lord Jesus Christ condemned such an attitude when
He commanded those who follow Him to seek first the
kingdom of God and His righteousness; and He promised
them that all these needful things should be added unto them.
He emphasized the stupidity of spending a lifetime in the
pursuit of wealth and the accumulation of earthly possessions
at the sacrifice of more important things when He asked,
"What shall it profit a man, if he shall gain the whole world,
and lose his own soul?" (Mark 8:36). There are men who
think themselves too clever to sell any piece of property

without realizing a profit on their investment, but who set a very poor price on their souls. One night of pleasure, one word of approval from godless men, is the pittance for which they sell the immortal part of themselves. There are women who spend hours every week and more money than they can afford on clothes and beauty treatments who never have a moment for the study of God's Word and the contemplation of His love with which to increase the soul's beauty. While they hang in their closets more dresses than they need, they neglect to provide for themselves a robe of righteousness.

The body goes to dust but the soul lives forever. The residences which men build for themselves on the earth grow old and deteriorate in value. Fire consumes them; age destroys them. Death comes and takes away the ones who dwell in them. Infinitely more important is a "building of God, an house not made with hands, eternal in the heavens" (II Corinthians 5:1).

How much happier we would be if, viewing our lives in the light of eternity, we would obey the Word of the Lord, "Lay not up for yourselves treasures upon earth, where moth and rust doth corrupt, and where thieves break through and steal: but lay up for yourselves treasures in heaven, where neither moth nor rust doth corrupt, and where thieves do not break through nor steal" (Matthew 6:19, 20).

> O Morning Star! how fair and bright
> Thou beamest forth in truth and light,
> O Sovereign meek and lowly!
> Thou Root of Jesse, David's Son,
> My Lord and Bridegroom, Thou hast won
> My heart to serve Thee solely!
> Jesus! Jesus
> Fair and glorious, all victorious,
> Rich in blessing,
> Rule and might o'er all possessing!
>
> Thou heavenly Brightness! Light divine!
> O deep within my heart now shine,
> And make Thee there an altar!

Fill me with joy and strength to be
Thy member, ever joined to Thee,
In love that cannot falter;
Jesus! Jesus
Doth possess me; turn and bless me;
Here in sadness
Eye and heart long for Thy gladness!
—*Philipp Nicolai*

* * *

ISOLATIONIST

MAN is not self-sufficient. Some men like to think they are, but no one can find in himself the answer to his own hunger of heart and longing of soul. The man who is self-reliant in the sense that he relies solely upon his own skill and strength and power leans upon a weak support, however clever and brilliant he may be. The man who seeks to satisfy the craving of his heart with *things* finds the hunger still unappeased. Money, land, stocks and bonds cannot meet man's deepest needs. Books, pictures, music—these are not sufficient. Even the man who relies upon friends for the satisfaction of the desire of his soul for companionship and for understanding to meet the problems and sorrows of life finds them insufficient.

The psalmist has expressed the need of men's hearts in the words, "My soul thirsteth for God, for the living God" (Psalm 42:2). The soul is immortal and only the immortal God can quench its thirst. Jesus Christ spoke about a rich man who said to his soul, "Soul, thou hast much goods laid up for many years; take thine ease, eat, drink, and be merry" (Luke 12:19). His barns were full of produce; his crops had been good. He had made his fortune, but he was a fool to attempt to satisfy his soul with those things. The human soul cannot slake its thirst at the wells of the world.

Man can come into a soul-satisfying acquaintance with God

only through the Lord Jesus Christ. He is God manifest in the flesh. "He that hath seen me hath seen the Father" (John 14:9), said Jesus Christ. Christ is God revealed and manifest to meet the needs of men. Jesus said of Himself, "Whosoever drinketh of the water that I shall give him shall never thirst; but the water that I shall give him shall be in him a well of water springing up into everlasting life" (John 4:14). The human heart pants after God as the hart panteth after the water brooks (Psalm 42:1). God's invitation to man is, "Let him that is athirst come. And whosoever will, let him take the water of life freely" (Revelation 22:17).

> As pants the hart for cooling streams
> When heated in the chase,
> So longs my soul, O God, for Thee
> And Thy refreshing grace.
>
> For Thee, my God, the living God,
> My thirsty soul doth pine;
> O when shall I behold Thy face,
> Thou Majesty divine!
>
> Why restless, why cast down, my soul?
> Trust God; and He'll employ
> His aid for thee, and change these sighs
> To thankful hymns of joy.
>
> Why restless, why cast down, my soul?
> Hope still; and thou shalt sing
> The praise of Him who is thy God,
> Thy Saviour and thy King.
>
> —*Psalm 42*
> *(Tate and Brady's New Version, 1696)*

* * *

ACTIONS SPEAK

JOHN the Baptist, that remarkable man, was thrown into prison by Herod because of his faithful preaching and courageous denunciation of sin. To him in the darkness of the dungeon came various reports about Christ, and John who had pointed to Jesus and cried with such certainty, "Behold the Lamb of God, which taketh away the sin of the world," confused and perplexed and discouraged, now sent to Him from jail, asking, "Art thou he that should come?" The answer of the Lord Jesus Christ was divinely positive. He did not insist loudly that indeed He was the Messiah nor send a message of rebuke to John because he had presumed to doubt His deity. He answered the question with no declaration of His own Messiahship at all. He said simply, "Go and shew John again those things which ye do hear and see" (Matthew 11:4).

John's messengers had had an opportunity to observe the miraculous and divine power of Christ. They had been present as He gave sight to the blind, made the lame walk, cleansed lepers, unstopped deaf ears, raised the dead, and preached the Gospel to the poor. What better answer could Christ have given to John's question than the answer of His life and work? Every act of the Lord Jesus proclaimed His deity.

The outward action of a man's life is the best indication of what he really is. The Lord stressed this truth. "Even so every good tree bringeth forth good fruit; but a corrupt tree bringeth forth evil fruit. A good tree cannot bring forth evil fruit, neither can a corrupt tree bring forth good fruit. . . . Wherefore by their fruits ye shall know them" (Matthew 7:17-20). A man is bound to manifest outwardly by his words and his actions what he is in his heart, for out of the heart are the issues of life (Proverbs 4:23), and as a man thinketh in his heart, so is he (Proverbs 23:7).

Some men say, "It does not matter what my creed is so long as I live right." The truth is that no man who has a bad creed can be a good man. That which a man believes in his heart affects the course of his outward life. James says, "Shew me thy faith without thy works, and I will shew thee my faith by my works" (James 2:18). The only way the heart of a man is apparent to others is by the works of his life.

When the saving grace of God transforms the heart of a man it transforms his life. Men may scoff at the grace of God and profess to doubt the miracle of the new birth, but skeptics have no answer to the proof of God's power and the evidence of the new birth when it is manifest in a transformed, godly life.

> Christian, rise, and act thy creed,
> Let thy prayer be in thy deed;
> Seek the right, perform the true,
> Raise thy work and life anew.
>
> Hearts around thee sink with care;
> Thou canst help their load to bear,
> Thou canst bring inspiring light,
> Arm their faltering wills to fight.
>
> Let thine alms be hope and joy,
> And thy worship God's employ;
> Give Him thanks in humble zeal,
> Learning all His will to feel.
>
> Come then, Law divine, and reign,
> Freest faith assailed in vain,
> Perfect love bereft of fear,
> Born in heaven and radiant here.
>
> —F. A. Rollo Russell

* * *

THE PROOF OF THE PUDDING

This is the day of the so-called "scientific" mind, the generation of those who must have proof before they will accept a truth. How often do we hear someone say, "I cannot take anything on faith. You have to prove something to me before I believe it." With these words some people explain their refusal to accept the salvation which God offers, since this salvation is by faith.

As a matter of fact, even in the realm of science faith goes before proof. The scientist believes—that is, he has faith — that certain chemicals mixed together will produce certain results. Therefore, in the laboratory he mixes the chemicals to prove by experiment whether the thing he believes is true. A physician has faith that a certain drug has power to cure a disease and because he believes the drug has power he tries the drug in the treatment of the disease.

God asks us to apply this same sort of faith in the realm of the spiritual. His invitation is, "O taste and see that the Lord is good" (Psalm 34:8). All God asks is that we try Him. Such a challenge from the God of the universe to the race which He created should appeal to the "scientific" mind.

When one scientist has definitely demonstrated that a certain fact is scientifically true, other scientists accept his proof and go on from there in their research without having to reprove the truth which he has established. It is not necessary to establish proof of the fact that the blood of the Lord Jesus Christ can change men's hearts and give them new natures. This eternal truth has been proved in the lives of countless thousands. In any other field than the spiritual, the "scientific" mind would accept such overwhelming evidence without a moment's hesitation. Yet in the realm of the spiritual, men not only decline to believe that which has been proved thousands of times by others but they also refuse to make the experiment themselves. "Believe on the Lord Jesus Christ, and thou shalt be saved" (Acts 16:31), says the Bible, but the "modern, wise, and scientific" mind says, "You will have to prove that to me." The proof lies in believing. When we believe we prove.

> Art thou weary, art thou languid,
>   Art thou sore distressed?
> "Come to Me," saith One, "and coming,
>   Be at rest."
>
> Hath He marks to lead me to Him,
>   If He be my guide?
> "In His feet and hands are wound-prints,
>   And His side."

Is there diadem, as Monarch,
   That His brow adorns?
"Yea, a crown, in very surety,
   But of thorns."

If I find Him, if I follow,
   What His guerdon here?
"Many a sorrow, many a labor,
   Many a tear."

If I still hold closely to Him,
   What hath He at last?
"Sorrow vanquished, labor ended,
   Jordan passed."

If I ask Him to receive me,
   Will He say me nay?
"Not till earth and not till heaven
   Pass away."

Finding, following, keeping, struggling,
   Is He sure to bless?
Saint, apostle, prophets, martyrs,
   Answer, "Yes!"

—Stephen the Sabaite

*   *   *

DREAMING

JOSEPH was a dreamer. There is nothing wrong with dreaming the right sort of dreams if dreams do not become the whole end of life.

Of course, Joseph's dreams were prophetic. They were sent to him by God as a promise of what he should become. He dreamed that the sun and the moon, representing his father and mother, and eleven stars, representing his brothers, bowed down to his star. He dreamed he and his family were gathering grain in the field together and that the sheaves of his mother and father and brethren bowed down to his sheaf. It is interesting and significant that these prophetic indications of the glory that lay ahead of Joseph should have shaped themselves into dreams about such simple things — stars and sheaves of grain. These were the things with which Joseph was familiar and with which he lived. Through the clear Eastern night, as he sat outside his father's tent or kept watch with his brothers over his father's flocks, he became familiar with the moon and stars. Up before day, he had often watched the sunrise. His life was largely occupied with the planting, the cultivation, and the harvesting of crops.

Men's dreams are an indication of their interest and a key to their lives. The things upon which your thoughts dwell indicate what you are. The ambitions which you set for yourself measure the quality of your character. The desires of the heart shape the course of the life. The man who thinks evil thoughts and dreams evil dreams will bring forth a crop of evil deeds. No wonder, then, that the Word of God admonishes, "Whatsoever things are true, whatsoever things are honest, whatsoever things are just, whatsoever things are pure, whatsoever things are lovely, whatsoever things are of good report; if there be any virtue, and if there be any praise, think on these things" (Philippians 4:8). The man with an impure heart cannot live a pure life. The man whose impulses and desires are sinful will lead a sinful life, but through grace he may receive a cleansing of heart, for the blood of Jesus Christ, God's Son, cleanses from all sin (I John 1:7).

> Go, dreamer, seek thy dream,
> And having found it, hold;
> The word has need of dreams
> That are not weighed in gold.
>
> Dream high! — and having dreamed,
> To thine own dream be true;
> Count not the cost, for dreams are things
> Worth many a cup of rue.

So dream that when the night come
Unto thy brief of days,
A dream goes singing down the winds
Of everlasting ways.
                              —*Florence Wilson Roper*

*   *   *

PERSPECTIVE

Two men looking on the same scene behold entirely different things. The story goes that two travelers stood together on a mountain peak looking down into the valley just as the first rays of the sun fired the clouds above which they were standing. One man exclaimed at the beauty of the scene. The other said, "This is the first time I ever looked down on a buzzard that was flying." One man was enraptured with the beauty of the dawn. The other man saw a buzzard.

What we are influences what we see. That which occupies our mind shapes our outlook. Looking at a magnificent public building, the architect looks for details of size and proportion and architectural style. The landscape artist notices the shrubbery set against the building. The housekeeper is conscious of the fact that the steps are dirty.

The prophet and his servant were surrounded by their enemies. The servant saw the horses and chariots and the soldiers that had come to take them prisoners. The prophet saw God's horses and chariots and heavenly soldiers. The servant of the prophet was frightened by what he saw. The prophet's vision made him bold and confident, and he prayed for his servant, saying, "Lord, I pray thee, open his eyes, that he may see" (II Kings 6:17). The Lord heard the prayer and the servant was given the spiritual vision of the prophet.

Jesus said, "Blessed are the pure in heart: for they shall see God" (Matthew 5:8). Only the man whose heart is pure can see God. The man whose heart is sinful and impure is blind to the presence of God. His sight is so filled with that which is ugly and debased that he has no time to catch a glimpse of the pure and holy. The man who is occupied solely with the temporal and physical cannot be expected to see the spiritual and eternal. "But the natural man receiveth not the things of the Spirit of God: for they are foolishness unto him: neither can he know them, because they are spiritually discerned" (I Corinthians 2:14).

> Blessed are the eyes that see
> The things that you have seen,
> Blessed are the feet that walk
> The ways where you have been.
>
> Blessed are the eyes that see
> The agony of God,
> Blessed are the feet that tread
> The paths His feet have trod.
>
> Blessed are the souls that solve
> The paradox of pain,
> And find the path that, piercing it,
> Leads through to peace again.
> —*G. A. Studdert Kennedy*

* * *

CHRISTENDOM AND CHRISTIANITY

COLUMNISTS and commentators complain that our "Christian civilization" has apparently failed because we have not established equity and brotherhood, justice and peace upon the earth. Our Western civilization, they declare, has in theory committed itself to the principles set forth in the teachings of Christ, but in fact it has not attained them.

These men have overlooked, as have many other people in these last few years, the fact that there is a difference between Christendom and Christianity, between having accepted the teachings of Christ as the proper basis for ideal human relationships and having become a Christian.

Thoughtful and benevolent men are compelled to recognize in the truths which Christ taught, in the example which He set, and in the instruction which He gave to His disciples, the noblest conception and the finest pattern of life. But the mental acceptance of these things does not make a man a Christian. Nor does the fact that a nation recognizes in its constitution some of the truths which Christ taught make that nation a Christian nation, nor does it establish His kingdom upon the earth. Christ Himself taught definitely that to become a Christian one must be born again (John 3:3). We do not grow into the kingdom of our Lord. We are born into it by simple trusting faith in Christ and by acceptance of Him as personal Saviour and as Lord of our lives. We do not become Christians when we accept the truth of His teachings. We become Christians when we accept Him, who is the Truth.

We do not hear much preaching these days on the new birth. There is a great need for it. "Ye must be born again" (John 3:7), says Christ, and until a man is born again he has no right to call himself a Christian, however much intellectual assent he may give to the truth of Christ's teachings. As for attaining a state of absolute equity and justice and final peace upon the earth, that is something we shall never experience until the Prince of Peace Himself comes to reign over the earth. Then the kingdoms of this world will become in reality the kingdoms of our Lord and of His Christ (Revelation 11:15).

> The King shall come when morning dawns,
>   And light triumphant breaks;
> When beauty gilds the eastern hills,
>   And life to joy awakes.
>
> Not as of old a little child
>   To bear, and fight, and die,
> But crowned with glory like the sun
>   That lights the morning sky.

O brighter than the rising morn
  When He, victorious, rose,
And left the lonesome place of death,
Despite the rage of foes—

O brighter than the glorious morn
Shall this fair morning be,
  When Christ, our King, in beauty comes,
  And we His face shall see!

The King shall come when morning dawns,
  And light and beauty brings:
Hail, Christ, the Lord! Thy people pray,
  "Come quickly, King of kings."
                              —*Greek Hymn*

*   *   *

FAITH AT REST

SOME people believe Christ. Some believe on Him. When Jesus was here on earth some believed that He was the Messiah. They took Him at His word. Their belief was strengthened by the evidence of the miracles He performed and by the life He lived. They believed Him. But, when He talked about sacrifice and suffering and hardship, they turned back from following Him. They believed Him, but they did not trust their lives to Him nor risk their future to His leadership.

Some people today believe Him to the extent that they accept the words which He spoke as truth. They believe He is the Son of God. They do not doubt His deity. They give intellectual assent to His truth, but they do not commit their lives to Him nor prove that they believe Him by obedience and surrender to His will.

Believing on Jesus is another matter altogether than believing Him. To believe on Jesus means to trust Him completely, not only to accept what He said as truth, but also to believe Him enough to commit oneself eternally to His keeping. To believe on Him is to make Him, who is the "sure foundation," the foundation on which our lives are built, the center about which the acts and thoughts and ambitions and desires of our lives are gathered. To believe on Jesus means to cling to Him as the support and stay of life. It means that we, conscious of our own weakness, rely on Him and depend upon His truth and power. To believe on the Lord Jesus Christ means to depend upon Him as a man escaping from a burning building depends upon the ladder which he descends. It is to depend upon Him as the pilot of a plane "flying blind" depends upon his instruments and the radio beam.

"Believe on the Lord Jesus Christ, and thou shalt be saved" (Acts 16:31). It is not enough simply to believe Him. We must in faith trust ourselves *to* Him, must believe *on* Him.

> Approach, my soul, the mercy seat,
>   Where Jesus answers prayer;
> There humbly fall before His feet,
>   For none can perish there.
>
> Thy promise is my only plea,
>   With this I venture nigh;
> Thou callest burdened souls to Thee,
>   And such, O Lord, am I.
>
> Bowed down beneath a load of sin,
>   By Satan sorely pressed,
> By wars without and fears within,
>   I come to Thee for rest.
>
> Be Thou my shield and hiding place,
>   That, sheltered near Thy side,
> I may my fierce accuser face,
>   And tell him Thou hast died.
>
> O wondrous Love! to bleed and die,
>   To bear the cross and shame,
> That guilty sinners, such as I,
>   Might plead Thy gracious Name!

"Poor tempest-tossèd soul, be still;
  My promised grace receive":
'Tis Jesus speaks—I must, I will,
  I can, I do believe.

—John Newton

* * *

BLINDNESS—GOOD AND BAD

THERE are two kinds of blindness referred to in the forty-second chapter of Isaiah. One is the sort of blindness which the Lord came to heal (verse 7). The other is a blindness which the Lord looks upon and finds well pleasing to Him (verse 19). The first is a guilty blindness; the second is a God-honoring blindness.

There are some men who are spiritually blind. They are blind to their true condition. They do not comprehend the fact that they are sinners and need a Saviour. Their eyes have been blinded by the god of this world so that they do not realize that it is impossible for man in his own righteousness to please God. Instead of seeing their need of the righteousness of Christ they go about to establish their own righteousness (II Corinthians 4:4). They are blind to spiritual truth.

When Christ comes into life He gives sight. Spiritual darkness and night turn to day. Just as He opened the physical eyes of the blind man beside the road, so He gives spiritual sight to those who cry out to Him. He is the Light of the World, and He floods the life with light.

There is the other sort of blindness. It is blindness to the appeal and attraction of the world. Some men and women have caught a vision of the face of Christ—a vision so bright that their eyes have been blind to the lights of earth ever since. Their gaze is not fixed upon earthly things. Their glances are not trapped by the display of earth. Their eyes do not feast upon the tinsel of time. Their affection is fixed upon things above. The lust of the eye which is not of the

Father but of the world (I John 2:16) has no power over them. Their eyes are blind to fleeting, temporal sights. The man who looks long at the sun and then turns his eyes toward a candle flame cannot see it. The Christian whose gaze lingers upon the Light of the World becomes blind to the dim candles of a sinful age.

> Walk in the light! so shalt thou know
>   That fellowship of love
> His Spirit only can bestow
>   Who reigns in light above.
>
> Walk in the light! and thou shalt find
>   Thy heart made truly His
> Who dwells in cloudless light enshrined,
>   In whom no darkness is.
>
> Walk in the light! and thou shalt own
>   Thy darkness passed away,
> Because that light hath on thee shone
>   In which is perfect day.
>
> Walk in the light! and e'en the tomb
>   No fearful shade shall wear;
> Glory shall chase away its gloom,
>   For Christ hath conquered there.
>
> Walk in the light! thy path shall be
>   A path, though thorny, bright:
> For God, by grace, shall dwell in thee,
>   And God Himself is Light.
>
> —*Bernard Barton*

* * *

TOMBSTONES

JESUS CHRIST, so kind to sinners and so tender in dealing with human weakness, lashed out in vigorous language of stern reproach against the Pharisees: "Ye are like unto whited sepulchres . . . full of dead men's bones" (Matthew 23:27).

Judged by one standard they were very righteous, but their standard was their own standard, and their righteousness was self-righteousness. They were careful about their outward observance of all the laws and ceremonies. They were careful to observe fasts and often prayed—in public—but all their righteousness was outward. Their religion was a religion of "don't's" and "do's." It was all on the surface. They vigorously contended for the faith and took pride in its championship, but in their own hearts was no spiritual life. Their souls were corrupt and full of rottenness; their religion was a shell. Without spirituality their religion was not inward life but a garment of practice, clothing the outward man.

The Pharisees are still with us. They were not peculiar to Israel. Christianity today — even the most conservative orthodox Christianity — is blighted by some who have inherited the worst traits of Israel's self-righteous sect. They are proud of their peculiarities and thankful they are not like other men. They have a head knowledge of the Gospel and an outward practice of its righteousness in which they take great pride. Inwardly there is none of the abundant life of Christ, none of His passion for lost men, none of His love for sinners. They judge other men and women on the basis of the standards which they themselves have set up and their judgments are harsh and cruel and un-Christlike.

The man who is born of God will manifest in his outward actions, in his daily life, the indwelling life which he possesses, and his whole life will be warm and sweet. The outward practice will be right because the inward man is right, and through every relationship of his life will shine the light and warmth of God's Spirit which dwells within his heart. There will be none of the coldness and hardness and self-righteousness of the Pharisee. There will be in his life none of the coldness of marble monuments covering the corruption and death in the Pharisee's heart.

> Is there ambition in my heart?
>   Search, gracious God, and see;
> Or do I act a haughty part?
>   Lord, I appeal to Thee.

I charge my thoughts, be humble still,
  And all my carriage mild,
Content, my Father, with Thy will,
  And quiet as a child.

The patient soul, the lowly mind
  Shall have a large reward:
Let saints in sorrow lie resign'd,
  And trust a faithful Lord.

—*Isaac Watts*

*   *   *

A PRICE TO PAY

IT IS always wise to ask oneself, "To what results will this course of action lead me?" A consideration of the consequences rarely precedes the deed which ultimately produces a tragedy. One who considers the inevitable results of sin will pause before rushing headlong to his destruction.

Playing with fire, the boy does not behold in advance the charred and smoking ruins which will result from his carelessness. Taking his first drink, the youth does not see in the glass the reflection of the red-eyed drunkard he will become. Juggling his expense account or misappropriating a few dollars, the young businessman fails to consider the humiliation and tragedy looming ahead on the road of dishonesty as it leads him toward gray prison walls.

This is an important question, "What effect will this act have on me today?" but definitely more important is the question, "What will be the final result of this act?"

In the time of the Prophet Jeremiah the nation of Judah had almost completely forgotten God. Enamored of the idolatry of neighboring countries, nobility and common people alike had become corrupt and wicked. Moral conditions were growing worse all the time. But, in those days, as always, God had a faithful few who did not follow the popular trend. Jeremiah was one of these. Alarmed by the blindness of the people to the impending national destruction, crying out against the popular sins of his day, he sought to warn them of the results of their course of life. Watching the people listen gladly to false prophets who promised peace and prosperity and blessing, Jeremiah asked them this question: "What will ye do in the end?" He lived to see the answer to his own question. In the end their city was destroyed. In the end they were slain or taken captive.

Sin always brings destruction in its wake. You may seem to get by with the violation of God's law today, but the "wages of sin is death." You may hide your sin from others now, but what will you do in the end when you come to stand in the presence of God, from whom nothing is hid?

> The day of wrath, that dreadful day,
> When heaven and earth shall pass away!
> What power shall be the sinner's stay?
> How shall he meet that dreadful day?
>
> When, shriveling like a parchèd scroll,
> The flaming heavens together roll;
> And louder yet, and yet more dread,
> Swells the high trump that wakes the dead.
>
> O on that day, that wrathful day,
> When man to judgment wakes from clay,
> Be Thou, O Christ, the sinner's stay,
> Though heaven and earth shall pass away!
>
> —*Walter Scott*

* * *

TWO THRONES

THE picture in the book of Revelation of men standing before a great white throne being judged for the deeds done in the body is dramatic and terrifying. Men and women are crying for the mountains to fall upon them and hide them from the face of Him who sits upon the throne. Those who rejected the grace of God and refused His salvation are gathered, small and great, before His judgment seat.

The Bible speaks of another throne. It is called "the throne of grace" (Hebrews 4:16). They who approach this throne now will never have to stand before the other throne— the throne of judgment. The judgment throne is to be set up in the future. The throne of grace is now established. Men will come before the judgment throne full of fear. Men approach the throne of grace with confidence. "Let us therefore come boldly unto the throne of grace, that we may obtain mercy, and find grace to help in time of need," said Paul. This throne of grace is a place of blessing—"the mercy seat"—and there is a reason for the boldness with which we may approach it.

The sinner needs salvation. He can boldly plead the blood of the Lord Jesus Christ. That blood sprinkles the mercy seat. The blood was shed for his sin. God promises forgiveness of sin to all who trust in Christ. "Believe on the Lord Jesus Christ, and thou shalt be saved" (Acts 16:31). A sinner may rely boldly upon the promise of God and at the throne of grace obtain forgiveness of his sin.

Here He will restore to fellowship the Christian who has been unfaithful and fallen into temptation. "If we confess our sins, he is faithful and just to forgive us our sins, and to cleanse us from all unrighteousness" (I John 1:9), and here we find power and victory in the time of temptation, grace to help in time of need.

> Sweet is Thy mercy, Lord;
>   Before Thy mercy seat
> My soul, adoring, pleads Thy word,
>   And owns Thy mercy sweet.
>
> My need and Thy desires
>   Are all in Christ complete;
> Thou hast the justice truth requires,
>   And I Thy mercy sweet.
>
> Where'er Thy Name is blest,
>   Where'er Thy people meet,
> There I delight in Thee to rest,
>   And find Thy mercy sweet.

Light Thou my weary way,
  Lead Thou my wandering feet,
That while I stay on earth I may
  Still find Thy mercy sweet.

Thus shall the heavenly host
  Hear all my songs repeat
To Father, Son and Holy Ghost,
  My joy, Thy mercy sweet.
                    —*John S. B. Monsell*

* * *

REJECTED DIAGNOSIS

SOME people do not want to be told the truth. There is
many a mother who does not want to be told the truth about
her child. Her son is a neighborhood nuisance, a cheat, and
a liar, but you could not get her to believe it. "He is a good
little darling, and so badly misunderstood," she will say.

There are some people who do not want the truth about
their talents. I once knew a woman who thought she had
great gifts as a singer and that she possessed a marvelous
voice. She sang off key and her voice was most unpleasant,
but no one—not even her vocal teacher—could make her
believe it. She thought she was a great singer, and she would
not listen to anyone who tried to tell her the truth about
how bad a singer she was.

There are people who will not believe the truth about their
physical condition. Their physicians recognize serious symp-
toms and warn them that they must take care of themselves,
but they will not believe the doctors or follow their advice.

But there are infinitely more people who will not believe
the truth about their spiritual condition. Men do not like
to admit that they are sinners or that they need a Saviour.
Full of self-righteousness, they refuse to accept the truth
of God's Word when it says, "All have sinned, and come
short of the glory of God" (Romans 3:23). They are quite

satisfied with their own spiritual condition and do not welcome the diagnosis of Almighty God.

How sad that men prefer falsehood to fact, that they welcome wrong and reject right, that they turn from truth to error. How melancholy the condition of those who change the truth of God into a lie (Romans 1:25). The Lord Jesus came to the Jews proclaiming His deity, announcing His Messiahship. They rejected His claims and refused to accept Him. He told them the truth about Himself and the truth about themselves, and they did not believe either. "Because I tell you the truth, ye believe me not" (John 8:45), He said.

When we recognize the truth of His deity, we must also acknowledge our own sinfulness. If He is as He claimed to be, the Truth, we must believe Him when He says, "Except a man be born again, he cannot see the kingdom of God" (John 3:3).

> Lord of all pow'r and might,
> Father of love and light,
> Speed on Thy Word:
> O let the Gospel sound
> All the wide world around,
> Wherever man is found;
> God speed His Word.
>
> Lo, what embattled foes,
> Stern in their hate, oppose
> God's holy Word:
> One for His truth we stand,
> Strong in His own right hand,
> Firm as a martyr band;
> God shield His Word.
>
> Onward shall be our course,
> Despite of fraud or force;
> God is before;
> His Word ere long shall run
> Free as the noonday sun;
> His purpose must be done;
> God bless His Word.
>
> —*Hugh Stowell*

THE KNOCK AT THE DOOR

THERE is no tragedy like the tragedy of a missed opportunity. The world is filled with people who are failures because they failed to take advantage of an opportunity. There are men who had a chance to get an education, but who failed to avail themselves of it and who, therefore, have never been able to realize their full possibilities since their minds are untrained and their talents undeveloped. There are others who failed to grasp opportunities suddenly thrust upon them whereby they might have secured fortune and prominence. Shakespeare has this to say about opportunities:

> There is a tide in the affairs of men,
> Which, taken at the flood, leads on to fortune;
> Omitted, all the voyage of their life
> Is bound in shallows and in miseries.

Some men are more fortunate than others. They neglect the first opportunity, and they are given another. To some men opportunity after opportunity is offered and none are taken advantage of.

Saddest of all neglected opportunities is the opportunity of salvation. God gives a man an opportunity to prepare for eternity, and he neglects it. Sometimes in His divine mercy innumerable opportunities are offered, but there comes a time when the last opportunity slips by and a soul goes into eternity unprepared and without hope.

When asked to trust Christ as their Saviour some say, "Not today; another time." They squander this opportunity and impose on God for another. The Word of God says, "Behold, now is the accepted time; behold, now is the day of salvation" (II Corinthians 6:2). There is now an opportunity. Tomorrow there may not be one. Life is uncertain and God's opportunities are fleet of wing. The wise man seizes the present opportunities.

The bodies of some of the men who lost their lives in

the attack of the Japanese upon Pearl Harbor were recovered from the sunken vessels. One of the Red Cross nurses helping to prepare the bodies for burial came upon the corpse of her own brother. In his hand was clasped his New Testament. In the back was printed, "I accept the Lord Jesus as my own personal Saviour," and in the blank provided underneath, the young man had signed his name. The nurse took the Testament and underneath his name she wrote her own, signifying that she had accepted her dead brother's Christ, thankful that he had seized his opportunity to prepare for eternity, and determined not to miss hers.

> Lo! on a narrow neck of land,
> 'Twixt two unbounded seas, I stand,
>   Secure, insensible:
> A point of time, a moment's space,
> Removes me to that heavenly place,
>   Or shuts me up in hell.
>
> O God, mine inmost soul convert,
> And deeply in my thoughtful heart
>   Eternal things impress:
> Give me to feel their solemn weight,
> And tremble on the brink of fate,
>   And wake to righteousness.
>
> Be this my one great business here,
> With serious industry and fear
>   Eternal bliss to insure;
> Thine utmost counsel to fulfill,
> And suffer all Thy righteous will,
>   And to the end endure.
>
> Then, Saviour, then my soul receive,
> Transported from this vale, to live
>   And reign with Thee above,
> Where faith is sweetly lost in sight,
> And hope in full, supreme delight,
>   And everlasting love.
>
> —*Charles Wesley*

*   *   *

"I Am the Door"
John 10:9

ONLY ONE DOOR

"I AM the door," said Jesus (John 10:7). He was not talking about the door of a beautiful palace. He was not speaking of the great doors of the Temple in Jerusalem. He had no lofty portals in mind. "I am the door of the sheepfold," He said. How amazing is the humility and condescension of the Lord, that He who is the God of glory should describe Himself in such humble, simple terms! He was talking to men who knew the habits and customs of sheep and shepherds. The sheep entered the fold at night for safety and protection from wild beasts. He was describing Himself, therefore, as the door to safety and security.

He is the means of entrance into the safety of eternal life. He is the only way by which men may enter. Some are trying to go in through good works. By their own efforts they are trying to climb a wall too high for them to top. Some try to enter through the practice of the Golden Rule, some by way of church membership, but Christ says, "I am the way, the truth, and the life: no man cometh unto the Father, but by me" (John 14:6).

There are no armed guards to keep poor ordinary folk out. There are no alms boxes fastened to the portal. No fine clothes are necessary. No cards of admission are demanded. Christ has described Himself as a door so humble that no man need feel too poor and vile to pass through. It is a low door, so low that a man cannot go through with his head held high. The stiff neck must bow if he would pass through this door.

We enter into salvation through Christ. We do not merit it. We cannot deserve it. We simply step through the Door by faith. There are not a half-dozen ways out of sin into eternal life. There is only one Way. Christ is not *a* door. He is *the* Door—the Door by which any man may enter in.

Thou art the Way: to Thee alone
From sin and death we flee;
And he who would the Father seek
Must seek Him, Lord, by Thee.

Thou art the Truth: Thy Word alone
True wisdom can impart;
Thou only canst inform the mind,
And purify the heart.

Thou art the Life: the rending tomb
Proclaims Thy conquering arm;
And those who put their trust in Thee
Nor death nor hell shall harm.

Thou art the Way, the Truth, the Life;
Grant us that way to know,
That truth to keep, that life to win,
Whose joys eternal flow.

—*George W. Doane*

* * *

FOUR DIMENSIONS

GOD'S love is four-dimensional. It extends through time and space. Paul speaks of the length and the breadth and the depth and the height of the love of God as that which passeth knowledge (Ephesians 3:18, 19). It is so wonderful, so profound, so remarkable that the human mind cannot comprehend it, understand it, analyze it.

God's love is long. It is as long as eternity. From before the foundation of the world God loved man yet uncreated. In the mind of God a plan was made for man's redemption. We are told that Jesus Christ was as a Lamb slain before the foundation of the world (Revelation 13:8). God's love is eternal, unfailing. Whom He loves He loves unto the end.

It is a broad love. It is broad enough to include all men of every age and race and condition. God's love embraces the most unattractive and the most unlovely. It is a love as broad as "whosoever," for God's love sent His Son "that whosoever believeth in him should not perish, but have everlasting life" (John 3:16), and the invitation is: whosoever will, let him come (Revelation 22:17).

God's love is deep—deep enough to reach down into the depths of man's need and man's depravity. It is extended down to the poor sinner who needs forgiveness and salvation from sin.

God's love is high—higher than the thoughts of man can soar, higher than the dreams of man can reach, high enough to raise a man to sonship with God. "Behold, what manner of love the Father hath bestowed upon us, that we should be called the sons of God," John cries (I John 3:1). It is a love so high that it can raise a sinner to eternal fellowship with the Most High God. It is as high as heaven itself, for it puts redeemed sinners on golden streets.

No wonder that it passeth knowledge—this love that manifests itself so perfectly in Christ, who loved us and gave Himself for us! Any man who could understand the love of God could understand God, for God is love (I John 4:16).

> O love of God, how strong and true,
> Eternal, and yet ever new;
> Uncomprehended and unbought,
> Beyond all knowledge and all thought.
>
> O heavenly love, how precious still,
> In days of weariness and ill,
> In nights of pain and helplessness,
> To hear, to comfort, and to bless!
>
> O wide-embracing, wondrous love,
> We read thee in the sky above;
> We read thee in the earth below,
> In seas that swell, and streams that flow.
>
> We read thee best in Him who came
> To bear for us the cross of shame,
> Sent by the Father from on high,
> Our life to live, our death to die.

O love of God, our shield and stay
Through all the perils of our way;
Eternal love, in Thee we rest,
Forever safe, forever blest.

—Horatius Bonar

*　　*　　*

WORDS! WORDS! WORDS!

IT WAS Spurgeon who said, "That which lies in the well
of your thought will come up in the bucket of your speech."
The Bible states the same truth more simply: "Out of the
abundance of the heart the mouth speaketh" (Matthew 12:
34). A man shows what he is by what he says. It was said
of Jesus Christ, "Never man spake like this man" (John
7:46). That He was the sinless Son of God was proved
by His words. Never an inaccurate or false word fell from
His lips. He spoke with the voice of divine authority and
the power of His words proved the power of the Speaker.
The word of the Lord of life brought forth a dead man
from the tomb. The word of the omnipotent God of the
universe silenced the tempest and calmed the sea. The word
of the sinless Son of God cast out demons from the bodies
of men and His word defeated Satan who sought to tempt
Him in the wilderness.

His word revealed a measure of values beyond the conception of the mind of sinful man. These were the standards
He set: that greatness abounds in service; that man's chief
concern should not be in the accumulation of things; that
outward appearance is not so important as the inward heart.

The most brilliant word of the greatest philosophers of
the generations, the highest truths uttered by the founders
of the religious systems of the world dim when compared
with the glorious light of His utterances.

Others suggest paths of ethical conduct and try to point out a way of life. Only God's Son says, "I am the way."

Others are seekers after the truth and professed teachers of it. Only Jesus Christ says, "I am the truth."

Others offer suggestions as to how to secure the most from life. Only Jesus Christ says, "I am the life."

Others with phrases of their philosophy attempt to enlighten the minds of men. Only Jesus Christ says, "I am the light of the world."

Wisdom of God, we would by Thee be taught;
Control our minds, direct our ev'ry thought;
Knowledge alone life's problems cannot meet;
We learn to live while sitting at Thy feet.

Light of the world, illumine us we pray;
Our souls are dark without Thy kindling ray,
Torches unlighted, of all rad'ance bare.
Touch them to flame, and burn in glory there!

Incarnate Truth, help us Thy truth to learn,
Prone to embrace the falsehood we would spurn,
Groping in error's maze for verity;
Thou art the Truth we need to make us free.

Unfailing love, we are so cold in heart,
To us Thy passion for the lost impart;
Give us Thy vision of the need of men;
All learning will be used in service then.

—*Bob Jones, Jr.*

* * *

THE MAGNETISM OF THE CROSS

Many years ago in England a man named Dodd wrote a commentary on the Bible. He was later convicted of a crime and sentenced to execution. After he had been hanged, the publishers realized that they could not sell a commentary under his name, and so they asked another learned gentleman, Dr. Coke, to sponsor the work, and it was published with his name prominently displayed on the flyleaf.

It is natural that a man who was hanged should leave behind him such an unsavory reputation that the people would not be attracted to his commentary on the Bible.

But what the gallows is in our modern day, such was the cross in the time of Christ. It was looked upon as we look upon the gibbet, not merely as an instrument of death, but as a sign of ignominy and disgrace. Crucifixion was the form of death reserved very largely for criminal slaves. To be sentenced to death upon the cross was to be marked with the stigma of crime and disgrace.

But note the wonders of God's supernatural grace and power! That very form of death which in the natural course of events would cause men to turn away in disgust or remember with repugnance the victim, is, in the case of the Lord Jesus, the very thing which attracts men to Him. He has forever glorified the instrument which would have debased another. Because He suffered on the cross, millions reverence the cross. It is lifted on church steeples, worn as ornaments.

Because He was lifted up upon the cross, men and women are attracted to Him. On the cross He revealed the fullest measure of God's love for sinners. In the humiliation of His death He showed Himself most royal. In His suffering, naked, bleeding, and physically repulsive, He appears most divinely attractive. It is through the preaching of the Gospel of His atoning death that sinners find forgiveness and men are drawn to Him, who said, "I, if I be lifted up from the earth, will draw all men unto me" (John 12:32).

> In the cross of Christ I glory,
>   Towering o'er the wrecks of time;
> All the light of sacred story
>   Gathers round its head sublime.

When the woes of life o'ertake me,
    Hopes deceive, and fears annoy,
Never shall the cross forsake me;
    Lo! it glows with peace and joy.

When the sun of bliss is beaming
    Light and love upon my way,
From the cross the radiance streaming
    Adds more luster to the day.

Bane and blessing, pain and pleasure,
    By the cross are sanctified;
Peace is there, that knows no measure,
    Joys that through all time abide.

                      —John Bowring

*   *   *

"IT IS FINISHED"

"It is finished" (John 19:30). Thus Christ hanging on the cross cried with a loud voice before He gave up the ghost. The agony of the crucifixion was over—the awful suffering first under the heat of the sun, and then in the darkness which God drew like a curtain about Calvary. He had hung there, racked with pain. He had been mocked and insulted. Now the time of release was come. Into His Father's hands He commended His spirit and died (Luke 23:46).

But more was finished than the physical suffering. Redemption's work was done. He had finished paying the penalty of sin. He had finished the task which would make sinful man acceptable to a sinless God. He had completed the work of salvation. There was nothing more which could be done. He had suffered, the Just for the unjust.

Some men do not realize how completely it was finished. There are those who still try to work out salvation for themselves. They are trying to make themselves acceptable unto

God by good deeds. When they sin, they seek to counterbalance that by an act of righteousness, hoping that God will take account of the good and overlook the bad. They labor fruitlessly, seeking to accomplish that which cannot be done "for by the works of the law shall no flesh be justified" (Galatians 2:16). They seek to do what has already been done — the work of salvation. Christ on the cross finished that work. Our salvation depends not upon what we do but upon what He has done. When we accept Him as our Saviour, when we by faith identify ourselves with Him, we are saved, for He "bare our sins in his own body on the tree" (I Peter 2:24). They were atoned for when He died. We are forever free from their guilt. Nothing remains to be done about them. He took care of every sin when He died. Forever and eternally "it is finished"!

> Cross of Jesus, cross of sorrow,
> Where the blood of Christ was shed,
> Perfect man on thee did suffer,
> Perfect God on thee has bled!
>
> Here the King of all the ages,
> Thron'd in light ere world could be,
> Robed in mortal flesh is dying,
> Crucified by sin for me.
>
> O mysterious condescending!
> O abandonment sublime!
> Very God Himself is bearing
> All the suffering of time!
>
> Evermore for human failure
> By His passion we can plead;
> God has borne all mortal anguish,
> Surely He will know our need.
>
>   —*James S. Simpson*

*   *   *

FREEDOM FOREVER

POSSIBLY none of the words of Christ are more often quoted than these: "And ye shall know the truth, and the truth shall make you free" (John 8:32). They lend their beauty to many a political speech and many an educational lecture. They gleam like brilliant gems amid the rubbish of many a sterile sermon. They are engraved on the walls of university libraries and carved over the doors of college chapels.

In one sense there is freedom in all truth. However, truth is arrived at in two different ways. Some truth comes by discovery; some truth by revelation. The scientist in his laboratory, by experiment and research, may discover truths in the realm of science. The biologist, the botanist, or the chemist may discover truths of natural law and use these truths to free man from the scourge of disease. The archaeologist may uncover truths from buried civilization and free men from false ideas about nations long since vanished. By the trial and error method many may attain to truth, and truth brings freedom from error.

Spiritual truth, however, comes by revelation from God Himself. God, who in Himself is the embodiment of all truth, reveals Himself to man in the Person of the Lord Jesus Christ, His Son. The truth of man's lost condition, the truth of the life hereafter, the truth of the Person and love of God is revealed in the Bible, the Word of God. Truth which man discovers for himself frees him from error, but only the truth which God reveals frees man from sin and its power and its penalty. The mind of many by searching cannot discover God, and only God in the Person of the Lord Jesus Christ is able to strike off the shackles of habit and sin and weakness which bind man body and soul. This eternal freedom which evades human discovery but comes as the gift of divine revelation is found in the Lord

Jesus Christ. He who said, "And ye shall know the truth, and the truth shall make you free," said of Himself, "I am the truth"; and only God's Son frees man from self, from his own sinful passions and tendencies, and from the condemnation of his sin.

Wonderful words, these, "The truth shall make you free," but completely realized only in Christ, the Incarnate Truth. "If the Son therefore shall make you free, ye shall be free indeed" (John 8:36).

> Lord of all being, throned afar,
> Thy glory flames from sun and star;
> Center and soul of every sphere,
> Yet to each loving heart how near!
>
> Sun of our life, Thy quickening ray
> Sheds on our path the glow of day;
> Star of our hope, Thy softened light
> Cheers the long watches of the night.
>
> Our midnight is Thy smile withdrawn;
> Our noontide is Thy gracious dawn;
> Our rainbow arch Thy mercy's sign;
> All, save the clouds of sin, are Thine!
>
> Lord of all life, below, above,
> Whose light is truth, whose warmth is love,
> Before Thy ever-blazing throne
> We ask no luster of our own.
>
> Grant us Thy truth to make us free,
> And kindling hearts that burn for Thee,
> Till all Thy living altars claim
> One holy light, one heavenly flame.
>
> —*Oliver W. Holmes*

* * *

A SURPRISED CONGREGATION

Wherever He was on the Sabbath, it was the custom of Christ to worship at the house of God. On one particular Sabbath (Mark 1:21-34) He amazed the congregation at the synagogue in Capernaum where He taught, because He spake with authority and not as the scribes to whom they were accustomed. But Christ did not only *speak* with authority; He demonstrated His authority—the authority of Deity Himself—by casting out an unclean spirit from a member of the congregation. The deity of Christ is clearly and explicitly taught and emphasized in the Word of God, and Christ Himself repeatedly, as on this occasion, by His miraculous power demonstrated His deity. When the demon was cast out of the man we are told that the congregation was "all amazed, insomuch that they questioned among themselves, saying, What thing is this? what new doctrine is this?" The demonstration of the eternal truth of His deity so amazed them that in their ignorance of the teaching of the Scripture they thought some new doctrine was being set forth.

It is possible to be in the house of worship and have an unclean spirit. It is possible to be a member of a church and a regular attendant at church worship and not be right of heart. All the ethical teaching and philosophy and emphasis on doctrine which the Church has to offer cannot cast out an unclean spirit, cannot give a man a newness of heart. Only the divine Christ is able to perform a regenerating miracle in the life of an individual. Church attendance is valuable and important. Christ Himself sets the example of attendance on public worship, but it is possible to come away from public worship still a slave to sin, unclean and lost. Only a personal meeting there or elsewhere with the Lord Jesus Christ and the acceptance of His divine authority as Lord and Saviour can accomplish the miraculous in the life of the individual.

> Come, sinners, to the Gospel feast;
> Let every soul be Jesus' guest;
> Ye need not one be left behind,
> For God hath bidden all mankind.

Sent by my Lord, on you I call;
The invitation is to all:
Come, all the world! come, sinner, thou!
All things in Christ are ready now.

Come, all ye souls by sin oppressed,
Ye restless wanderers after rest;
Ye poor, and maimed, and halt, and blind,
In Christ a hearty welcome find.

My message as from God receive;
Ye all may come to Christ and live:
O let His love your hearts constrain,
Nor suffer Him to die in vain.

See Him set forth before your eyes
That precious, bleeding sacrifice!
His offered benefits embrace,
And freely now be saved by grace.
—*Charles Wesley*

* * *

HURRAHS — HISSES!

THOSE few days from the triumphant entry of the Lord into Jerusalem to His crucifixion afford all the proof we need of the fact that popularity is a fleeting thing and that unregenerate man is a fickle and depraved creature.

When Christ entered Jerusalem He was acclaimed and applauded by the multitude. When He went out He was spat upon and jeered at by the mob. He rode into Jerusalem over the garments spread out before Him by the enthusiastic crowd. He went out of Jerusalem bearing a cross. As He was welcomed into the city they cried, "Blessed is he that cometh in the name of the Lord." As He was led out of the city they cried, "Away with him, away with him, crucify him." He was received into the city as if He were a conqueror and a king. He was led out of the city as if He were a malefactor and a criminal. When He came into Jerusalem, palm branches of victory were waved in salutation before Him. When He went out of Jerusalem, a crown of thorns was placed on His brow in mockery. He entered the city from the Mount of Olives surrounded by enthusiastic and admiring throngs. He went out of the city to the mount of execution, a condemned prisoner under guard. So overwhelming was the enthusiasm of His reception into Jerusalem that the Pharisees, His enemies, said, "Behold, the world is gone after him." So unpopular was He a few days later that not even the Roman governor, who found Him innocent, dared to risk the displeasure of the mob by setting Him free.

Our Lord, as He rode into Jerusalem amid the hosannas of the excited populace, knew they would reject and crucify Him. He had come into the world to die upon the cross, and the infinite Son of God was not deceived by the momentary swell of apparent popularity that greeted Him that day.

The Lord Jesus Christ knows all about the shallow and changeable human heart. He knows the fickleness of popular favor and the faithlessness of human friends. He saw a false friend betray, a trusted friend deny, cowardly friends follow afar off or flee in the hour of His trial.

It is a common occurrence in the history of a fallen race for fame to fade, friends to fail, and applause to die away, but the Lord Jesus Christ changes not nor faileth ever. He says in the hour of our loneliness and dejection and disappointment as in the time of joy and success and triumph, "Him that cometh unto me I will in no wise cast out." He is the one Friend who "sticketh closer than a brother," "the same yesterday, today, and for ever," infinite in love and compassion and understanding to all who trust in Him.

> Come, says Jesus' sacred voice,
> Come, and make My paths your choice;
> I will guide you to your home,
> Weary pilgrim, hither come!

Thou who, houseless, sole, forlorn,
Long hast borne the proud world's scorn,
Long hast roamed the barren waste,
Weary pilgrim, hither haste.

Ye who, tossed on beds of pain,
Seek for ease, but seek in vain;
Ye, by fiercer anguish torn,
In remorse for guilt who mourn—

Hither come! for here is found
Balm that flows for ev'ry wound,
Peace that ever shall endure,
Rest eternal, sacred, sure.

—Anna L. Barbauld

*   *   *

"Because I Live, Ye Shall Live Also"
John 14:19

CONTRASTS OF THE CHRIST

IT IS impossible to imagine any contrasts more definite than those which the Scripture makes between what the Lord Jesus Christ was and what He became.

He was God. John tells us, "In the beginning was the Word, and the Word was with God, and the Word was God" (John 1:1). He became man. "For verily he took not on him the nature of angels; but he took on him the seed of Abraham" (Hebrews 2:16). The most high God, the Creator of all things, took upon Himself the form of man, the creature.

He was the Lord of life. He "became obedient unto death, even the death of the cross" (Philippians 2:8).

He was the Master and Lord of the universe. "By him all things consist" (Colossians 1:17). But, He who was the Master became the servant. "The Son of man came not to be ministered unto, but to minister" (Matthew 20:28).

He was rich. All the riches of creation were His. John says, "Thou hast created all things, and for thy pleasure they are and were created" (Revelation 4:11). But, "though he was rich, yet for your sakes he became poor, that ye through his poverty might be rich" (II Corinthians 8:9). He walked the earth without a home or any possessions aside from the garments which He wore.

He was altogether lovely, the "rose of Sharon, and the lily of the valleys" (Song of Solomon 2:1), the fairest of ten thousand to the soul. But on the cross He became mis-shapen and horribly marred. "His visage was so marred more than any man, and his form more than the sons of men" (Isaiah 52:14), and Isaiah spoke prophetically of His terrible appearance in the hour of crucifixion when he wrote, "He hath no form nor comeliness; and when we shall see him, there is no beauty that we should desire him" (Isaiah 53:2).

What amazing contrasts! but no more amazing than the contrast of the hatred of sinful man for Him and His love for sinful man. Because He loved man, Christ became man, laid aside His glory, became poor, suffered death upon the cross. He, the God who loved so greatly the creatures which He made, was rejected and spurned and crucified by the very ones He came to save.

> "Unto you is born this day a Saviour,"
> Which is Jesus Christ, the wondrous Lord;
> Not a "teacher," not a "good example,"
> But the Son of God, the Living Word.
>
> No "philosopher," his fancies weaving,
> Warp of dreams and woof of visions vast,
> Not a "prophet," peering down the future,
> Not a "scholar," delving in the past.
>
> "Unto you is born this day a Saviour."
> Shine, O star! and shout, O angel voice!
> Unto you this precious gift is given;
> Sing, O earth! and all ye heavens, rejoice!
>
> Long the world has waited such a Saviour,
> Sunk in sin and torn by fear and doubt;
> Long in darkness groped for truth and wisdom;
> Glory, glory, now the light shines out!
>
> "Unto you is born this day a Saviour."
> Earth's one hope, the Life, the Truth, the Way;
> Mighty God and glorious Redeemer,
> Jesus Christ the Lord is born today.
>
> —*Annie Johnson Flint*

(Used by permission of Evangelical Publishers, Toronto and New York)

*   *   *

CORDS OF LOVE

It was Robert E. Lee who said, "Duty is the sublimest word in the English language." But though her name may be sublime, Duty's demands may be harsh and burdensome. "Must" is an unpleasant word. It sometimes speaks of harsh necessity. Jesus Christ said, "The Son of man *must* be lifted up" (John 12:34). God's Son *must* be nailed to the cross. Yet there was no drawing back from the obligation, no shirking the necessity. He must be lifted up because He loved, and love, eager to save poor sinners, made His death necessary. He must die because He loved. His submission to the will of God and His love for men were tangent at the cross. Not only in obedience to God's will, but also impelled by His love for sinners, He must die.

Christ's death fulfilled the prophecies of the Old Testament, but Jesus did not have to die because prophets had foreseen His death. The prophets foretold His death upon the cross because He *must* die upon the cross. Jesus Christ was as a "Lamb slain from the foundation of the world" (Revelation 13:8). In obedience to the will of the Father and because He loved men and willed to redeem them He *must* die. He had to die. It was necessary that the Son of Man be lifted up because the Son of Man came into the world to save sinners, and He must go to the cross to do the work of salvation. Because He was God, and God is love, He had to suffer.

He went to the cross willingly. He was bound to the tree not by the nails which impaled Him upon the beam. The God who hid in the earth the iron from which the nails were forged and made the tree of the cross grow from its seed could not have been held by the nails upon the wood against His will. He was bound there by the cords of His own divine love. He gave His life. No man took it from Him (John 10:18).

Thy habitation is eternity,
  Oh, high and holy One, who fillest space,
Yet Thou didst deign to leave Thine own abode
  And make with sinful man Thy dwelling place.
Thou, everlasting Father, Prince of Peace,
  To fleeting days and constant strife came down.

And Thou didst walk with men and share their toil,
  And feel their weariness and shed their tears;
Thou, mighty Counsellor, didst speak Thy words
  Of heaven's wisdom unto foolish ears;
And Thou wast patient with their ignorance,
  Their stubbornness, their pride, their unbelief;
Thou who art Life didst yield Thyself to death,
  Thou, pure and sinless, hung beside a thief.

  —*Annie Johnson Flint*

(Used by permission of Evangelical Publishers, Toronto and New York)

*　　*　　*

GOD OR NOT GOOD

Upon what charge was Jesus Christ sentenced to death; for what crime was He crucified? The answer is quite plainly stated in the Gospels; for making Himself equal with God, for claiming to be the Son of God.

The Jewish priests and the leaders of the people hated Christ because of His influence over the common people. They were jealous of His popularity. Their antagonism against Him was aroused because His holy eyes detected the hypocrisy of their own evil hearts and in words of truth and power He denounced them. They were determined to get rid of Him and in a trial which was one long mockery, He whose death they had predetermined upon was sentenced to die.

Either Jesus Christ is the Son of God or He was a fraud and an impostor and a blasphemer. The charges against Him were true. He had claimed to be God's Son. He identified Himself with the great God of eternity when He took to Himself the Name of the great eternal I AM, saying, "Before Abraham was, I am" (John 8:58). Seated at the well of Samaria and talking to the woman of Sychar about the Messiah that was to come, He declared, "I that speak unto thee am he" (John 4:26). Asked by the high priest at the trial, "I adjure thee by the living God, that thou tell us whether thou be the Christ, the Son of God" (Matthew 26:63), Christ answered, "Thou hast said," meaning, "As thou hast said, I am."

We are faced with this alternative: either Jesus Christ is God's Son or He was a blasphemer and a man who claimed to be that which He was not. No one can say logically that Jesus was a good man and nothing more. Either He is more than a good man—the God He claimed to be—or He was a deceiver and a wicked man.

> My dear Redeemer, and my Lord,
> I read my duty in Thy Word;
> But in Thy life the law appears,
> Drawn out in living characters.
>
> Such was Thy truth, and such Thy zeal,
> Such deference to Thy Father's will,
> Such love, and meekness so divine,
> I would transcribe and make them mine.
>
> Cold mountains and the midnight air
> Witnessed the fervor of Thy pray'r;
> The desert Thy temptations knew,
> Thy conflict and Thy victory, too.
>
> Be Thou my pattern; make me bear
> More of Thy gracious image here;
> Then God, the Judge, shall own my name
> Among the followers of the Lamb.
>
> —*Isaac Watts*

* * *

KING OF KINGS

"JESUS of Nazareth the king of the Jews." This title written by Pilate was nailed to the cross upon which Christ died. Pilate, evidently angered at the insistence of the Jewish leaders upon the death of Christ and possibly ashamed of his own weakness in giving way to them, in the words of the inscription jested at the Jews. The leaders of the people sent back a request to Pilate that the title be altered to read, "He said, I am King of the Jews" (John 19:21), and Pilate in his abrupt and angry reply, "What I have written I have written," betrayed his motive in setting up the inscription above the head of the Crucified. He implied by his words, "Behold this poor creature. He is a king, and over what a poor people does he reign!" As the reed placed in His hand was a mock scepter, as the crown of thorns upon His brow was a mock diadem, so Pilate by the inscription made the cross a mock throne.

Judah rejected her King but nowhere was He more kingly than upon the cross, and because He hung there in agony He shall some day sit upon the throne of David. He who endured the cross, despising the shame, shall reign over all nations. The brow crowned with thorns shall wear a diadem. The hand that held the reed and was nailed upon a cross shall grip a rod of iron and a scepter of power. Pilate wrote more truthfully than he knew that day. He is the King of the Jews, but the inscription was incomplete. God's full inscription will be written on His vesture and His thigh when He comes again in power to rule not Judah alone, but all the nations of the world as "King of kings, and Lord of lords" (Revelation 19:16).

> My God, I love Thee, not because
> I hope for heaven thereby,
> Nor yet because, if I love not,
> I must forever die.

Thou, O my Jesus, Thou didst me
 Upon the cross embrace:
For me didst bear the nails, and spear,
 And manifold disgrace.

Then why, O blessed Jesus Christ,
 Should I not love Thee well?
Not for the hope of winning heaven,
 Nor of escaping hell;

Not with the hope of gaining aught,
 Not seeking a reward;
But as Thyself hast lovèd me,
 O ever-loving Lord!

So would I love Thee, dearest Lord,
 And in Thy praise will sing;
Solely because Thou art my God,
 And my eternal King.
 —*Francis Xavier*

* * *

PERFECT OBEDIENCE

IT SEEMS strange to think of a God who is all powerful being compelled to do any certain thing. Yet the omnipotent God is by reason of His own righteousness compelled to a certain course. "Shall not the Judge of all the earth do right?" (Genesis 18:25). Because God is infinitely good, He cannot do evil. Because He is wholly righteous, God must be just. Because He promises, He must perform. Jesus Christ, God's Son, as He moved among men on several occasions, said, "I must." Incarnate Deity was bound by His own perfection to do the perfect will of the Father.

Coming into Jericho one day, Jesus stopped under a sycamore tree, into which a man, "little of stature," had climbed so that he might see Him over the heads of the crowd gathered around Him. Looking up, Jesus said, "Zacchaeus, make haste, and come down; for to day I must abide at thy house" (Luke 19:5).

Why must He? Because it was the will of the Father that Zacchaeus be saved. Jesus Christ had come into the world to save sinners. He was on His way to the cross to die for a lost world. His face was set like flint to go up to Jerusalem to die, but that day for a little while He must dine with Zacchaeus, so that Zacchaeus might feast with Him in glory.

There is no way to measure obedience. Obedience must hold in small things as well as in great or the perfection of obedience is shattered. God's truth is consistent in small matters as in great ones. Duty demands obedience in little tasks as well as in great deeds. Nothing is too trivial to be brought under the dominion of God's will. The obedient man knows that God not only orders the course of his whole life, but that each step is also definitely planned and directed (Psalm 37:23).

Jesus Christ exclaimed, "My meat is to do the will of him that sent me" (John 4:34). Because the Father willed it, He said that day in Jericho, "Zacchaeus . . . I must abide at thy house."

> When mother-love makes all things bright,
> When joy comes with the morning light,
> When children gather round their tree,
> Thou Christmas Babe,
> We sing of Thee!
>
> When manhood's brows are bent in thought,
> To learn what men of old have taught,
> When eager hands seek wisdom's key,
> Wise Temple Child,
> We learn of Thee!
>
> When doubts assail and perils fright,
> When, groping blindly in the night,
> We strive to read life's mystery,
> Man of the Mount,
> We turn to Thee!

When shadows of the valley fall,
When sin and death the soul appall,
One light we through the darkness see,
    Christ on the Cross,
    We cry to Thee!

And when the world shall pass away,
And dawns at length the perfect day,
In glory shall our souls made free,
    Thou God enthroned,
    Then worship Thee!

                          —*Tudor Jenks*

* * *

REMEMBERING OTHERS

THE character of our Lord Jesus Christ is nowhere more perfectly demonstrated than on the cross. He who died for sinners did not even in suffering on Calvary forget His own. He made provision for His mother and His friend, and what a tender provision it was! He had nothing on earth to give them. He died without property or possession. Though He made all things, He had no lands to leave. Though He, in creation, had hidden the gold in the hills, He died without money. Even His robe had been taken from Him and the soldiers were casting lots for it in the shadow of the cross. He had nothing of material value to leave to His mother and not even a keepsake to bequeath to His friend, so He gave them to each other—to the heartbroken mother, a son, upon whom the affection of a mother's heart could be lavished; to John, a mother, whose heart was capable of all the devotion a mother possesses.

His divine compassion showed itself in His prayer for those who crucified Him. "Father, forgive them; for they know not what they do" (Luke 23:34). His enemies, His tormentors, His persecutors came within the embrace of His divine compassion in the prayer.

It was not until He had made provision for His loved ones and prayed for His enemies that He thought of Himself. Then He cried, "I thirst" (John 19:28). Only thus does He give voice to the suffering of the flesh. "As a sheep before her shearers is dumb" (Isaiah 53:7), so He through the trial and the agony of the past hours had opened not His mouth in complaint or protest. The incarnate God gave only this brief cry to indicate the awful suffering of His flesh.

Was there ever anguish like His anguish? Yet was there ever one who died thus? His deity was so apparent as He died that the centurion in charge of the crucifixion was compelled to cry out, "Truly this man was the Son of God' (Mark 15:39).

> O love divine, that stoop'd to share
> Our sharpest pang, our bitt'rest tear,
> On Thee we cast each earth-born care,
> We smile at pain while Thou art near.
>
> Tho' long the weary way we tread,
> And sorrow crown each ling'ring year,
> No path we shun, no darkness dread,
> Our hearts still whisp'ring, "Thou art near."
>
> When drooping pleasure turns to grief,
> And trembling faith is chang'd to fear,
> The murm'ring wind, the quiv'ring leaf,
> Shall softly tell us Thou art near.
>
> On Thee we fling our burd'ning woe,
> O love divine, forever dear,
> Content to suffer, while we know,
> Living and dying, Thou art near.
>
> —*Oliver W. Holmes*

* * *

"IF'S" AND "BUT"

IF CHRIST be not risen from the dead, we can put no faith in the Bible as the true Word of God. If He be not risen, then Matthew, Mark, Luke, and John are all dealers in falsehood, and Paul is a deceiver and not to be trusted, for all these "have testified of God that he raised up Christ" (I Corinthians 15:15).

If Christ be not risen from the dead, the preaching of the apostles was vain and empty, founded on a quicksand of deceit or misunderstanding.

If Christ be not risen from the dead, all those who have preached the Christian doctrine of the resurrection in the succeeding nineteen centuries have been deluded. They have dreamed idle dreams without foundation, and spoken words of empty beauty void of truth.

If Christ be not risen from the dead, then all the dead of all the centuries sleep a soundless sleep from which there is no awakening. The night of death will never be shattered by the dawn of the resurrection day. They have been deceived by a mirage without substance who lie down to die looking forward to a resurrection from the dead.

If Christ be not risen from the dead, no man can stand in God's sight freed from sin and a possessor of eternal life. If He be not the Lord of life returned alive from the tomb, He is a mere man, dust these many generations and unable to impart life to the dusty dead of time.

"But now is Christ risen" (I Corinthians 15:20). There can be no doubt of that glorious fact. The reliable witnesses who saw Him after His resurrection, to whom He talked, who touched Him, who accepted food from His hand and ate it, give indisputable evidence that He is risen. The power of His resurrection life imparted to the lives of trusting thousands through all the years since that Easter Day attests His resurrection. "Now is Christ risen," and from His lips sounds the promise of resurrection to all who die in Him. To all His own, sleeping beneath the green of earth's valleys, the snows of its hillsides or the gray waves of its oceans, He speaks, "Because I live, ye shall live also" (John 14:19).

I know that my Redeemer lives;
What joy the blest assurance gives!
He lives, He lives, who once was dead;
He lives, my everlasting Head!

He lives, to bless me with His love;
He lives, to plead for me above;
He lives, my hungry soul to feed;
He lives, to help in time of need.

He lives, to grant me daily breath;
He lives, and I shall conquer death;
He lives, my mansion to prepare;
He lives, to bring me safely there.

He lives, all glory to His Name;
He lives, my Saviour, still the same;
What joy the blest assurance gives,
I know that my Redeemer lives!

—*Samuel Medley*

*   *   *

"I Know Whom I Have Believed"
II Timothy 1:12

SATISFACTION IN KNOWLEDGE

Great satisfaction is found in knowledge. To know thoroughly one's business or profession brings a sense of self-confidence. "Knowledge is power." We like to say with authority, "I know," but there are some people who spend their time wondering about things of which they could easily be sure.

Are you saved? "I don't think you can know about that until after you are dead," you may reply. "I hope I am saved." But you can know. The Bible is definite on the subject of salvation, and on the authority of God's Word you can know whether you are saved or not. "He that hath the Son hath life; and he that hath not the Son of God hath not life" (I John 5:12). "Believe on the Lord Jesus Christ, and thou shalt be saved" (Acts 16:31). God cannot lie, and the man who meets God's conditions can be assured that God keeps His promises. Jesus said, "Him that cometh to me I will in no wise cast out" (John 6:37). If you have come in faith to Christ and trusted Him as your Saviour, you can be sure that He saves you.

A long time ago somebody said, "Christianity is not a hope-so religion; it is a know-so religion." God would have men know whether or not they are saved. The Bible is full of warning to the sinner. God wants the sinner to know that abundant salvation is found in Jesus Christ so that he will turn to Christ and pass from death to life. God desires that the Christian have full assurance of his salvation and be able to say with conviction, "I know I am saved!"

Paul did not have any doubt about the matter. He said, "I know whom I have believed, and am persuaded that he is able to keep that which I have committed unto him against that day" (II Timothy 1:12). Every Christian can be just as positive as Paul since God's Holy Spirit indwelling us testifies to the reality of our salvation. "The Spirit himself beareth witness with our spirit, that we are the children of God" (Romans 8:16).

> How can a sinner know
>   His sins on earth forgiven?
> How can my gracious Saviour show
>   My name inscribed in heaven?
>
> What we have felt and seen,
>   With confidence we tell;
> And publish to the sons of men
>   The signs infallible.
>
> We who in Christ believe
>   That He for us hath died,
> We all His unknown peace receive,
>   And feel His blood applied.
>
> Exults our rising soul,
>   Disburdened of her load,
> And swells unutterably full
>   Of glory and of God.
>   —*Charles Wesley*

*   *   *

SEVENFOLD UNION

CHRIST and the believer are joined together in an association and relationship as wonderful as it is blessed. There are seven points in which the Christian is associated with his Lord.

The Christian is crucified with Christ (Galatians 2:20). When Christ died on the cross He paid our death penalty there. Christ hung there for us and in God's sight we were crucified with Him.

The Christian is quickened together with Him (Ephesians 2:5). The believer is alive with Christ. This is what Paul meant when he said, "For to me to live is Christ, and to die is gain" (Philippians 1:21). We are possessors of His eternal life. Because He lives, we live also (John 14:19).

The Christian is raised together with Christ (Ephesians 2:6). We are raised from the death of sin to walking in newness of life. When Christ rose from the tomb the resurrection of every child of God was as assured as if he had himself already risen.

The Christian is seated together in heavenly places with Christ (Ephesians 2:6). We enjoy heavenly privileges now: fellowship and communion with Him. We who are members of the body are represented in heaven by Christ who is the Head of the Church, and while we are yet here in the body on the earth, we are present in Him in the Court of Glory.

The Christian is a joint-heir with Christ (Romans 8:17). He is the heir of all things and He is our Elder Brother. We share in the family possessions. His heritage is jointly ours.

The Christian suffers with Christ (Romans 8:17). This is one phase of our relationship with Him which many of us would like to avoid, but the suffering which touches one member of a family touches all the family. No portion of the body suffers to itself and upon our relation with Christ in suffering depends our relation with Him in glory.

The Christian will be glorified together with Christ (Romans 8:17). Amazing mercy, love beyond our comprehension, that He who is worthy of all glory sees fit to share it with us who deserve none!

> Reality, reality,
> Lord Jesus Christ Thou art to me!
> From the spectral mist and the driving clouds,
> From the shifting shadows and phantom crowds,
> From unreal words and unreal lives,
> Where truth with falsehood feebly strives;
> From the passings away, the chance and change,
> Flickerings, vanishings, swift and strange,
> I turn to my glorious rest in Thee,
> Who art the grand Reality!

Reality, reality,
Lord Jesus Christ is crowned in Thee,
In Thee is every type fulfilled,
In Thee is every yearning stilled
For perfect beauty, truth and love:
For Thou art always far above
The grandest glimpse of our Ideal,
Yet more and more we know Thee real,
        And marvel more and more to see
        Thine infinite reality.

Reality, reality,
Lord Jesus Christ Thou art to me!
My glorious King, my Lord, my God,
Life is too short for half the laud,
For half the debt of praise I owe,
For this blest knowledge that "I know
The reality of Jesus Christ"—
Unmeasured blessing, gift unpriced!
        Will I not praise Thee when I see
        In the long noon of eternity
        Unveiled, Thy "bright reality"?
                    —*Frances Ridley Havergal*

*   *   *

THE END OF THE SEARCH

IT IS a strange thing how often people accuse other folk of doing the very thing of which they themselves are guilty. Zophar, one of the three men who came to "comfort" Job at the time of his sorrow and poverty, thought he knew all there was to know about God, yet he accused Job of being guilty of this same presumption and asked him, "Canst thou by searching find out God? canst thou find out the Almighty unto perfection?" (Job 11:7).

Man by searching can find out much about God. The physical universe reveals a great deal of the power and skill and wisdom of the Almighty. "The heavens declare the glory of God; and the firmament sheweth his handywork.

Day unto day uttereth speech, and night unto night sheweth knowledge" (Psalm 19:1, 2). The ordered regularity of the movements of the heavenly bodies reveal to the searching telescope of the astronomer the attribute of perfection which God possesses. The complexities in the patterns of nature speak of the infinite wisdom of God. The workings of God's moral law proclaim His justice. God "plants His foot upon the sea and rides upon the storm," and the searcher finds everywhere in creation evidence of Deity.

Finding out the Almighty to perfection is another thing. But Christ is the end of that search. The man who finds Christ finds the only perfect revelation of God. "He that hath seen me," said Jesus, "hath seen the Father" (John 14:9), and in Christ is found the only perfect revelation of Deity in all His attributes. "For in him dwelleth all the fulness of the Godhead bodily" (Colossians 2:9). He is God Incarnate, and the man who finds Christ finds God perfect in power, perfect in love, perfect in wisdom.

Job, looking forward with the eyes of faith through the years and seeing Him, exclaimed, "For I know that my redeemer liveth, and that he shall stand at the latter day upon the earth: and though after my skin worms destroy this body, yet in my flesh shall I see God" (Job 19:25, 26). When we find Christ we find God, and having our faith fixed on Him who is God the Redeemer, we share Job's assurance that some day, when our bodies have been transformed into the likeness of His glorious body, then in our flesh we shall see God.

> Majestic sweetness sits enthroned
> Upon the Saviour's brow;
> His head with radiant glories crowned,
> His lips with grace o'erflow.
>
> He saw me plunged in deep distress;
> He flew to my relief;
> For me He bore the shameful cross,
> And carried all my grief.

To Him I owe my life and breath,
    And all the joys I have;
He makes me triumph over death;
    He saves me from the grave.

To heaven, the place of His abode,
    He brings my weary feet;
Shows me the glories of my God,
    And makes my joy complete.

Since from His bounty I receive
    Such proofs of love divine,
Had I a thousand hearts to give,
    Lord, they should all be Thine.
                    —*Samuel Stennett*

*   *   *

THE SERENITY OF SURRENDER

THE Lord Jesus Christ is "the same yesterday, and to day, and for ever" (Hebrews 13:8). The man or woman whose faith is fixed in Him will be filled with a sense of complete confidence no matter how much conditions around him change. As the Prince of Peace, Christ is able to give peace of mind to those whose lives and thoughts are centered in Him.

The Christian should be unaffected by the variations in emotional temperature which occur around him. With a faith which is constant and unchanging, he walks serene amid the change and chaos of the world around. He maintains an inward peace however noisy the tumult and bloody the war which shakes the earth around him. When others are afraid he maintains the same restful attitude of trust which he felt when outward conditions were settled and quiet. He lives in the world but inwardly he is unaffected by its changing currents of thought, its seething emotions, its vain ideas. He is not swept off his feet by the current of popular opinion. His faith is fixed in a God who is eternal; his feet are set on the Rock of Ages.

The secret of maintaining such a state of life as this is found in the words of Isaiah: "Thou wilt keep him in perfect peace, whose mind is stayed on thee" (Isaiah 26:3). The man whose mind is constantly occupied with the affairs of this world, whose affection is fixed upon temporal things, is bound to be affected by the loss of earthly possessions and the changing conditions which give them changing values. Paul says to the Christian, "Set your affection on things above, not on things on the earth" (Colossians 3:2). Both life and peace are the possession of the man who is spiritually minded (Romans 8:6).

> Jesus, the very thought of Thee
>   With sweetness fills the breast;
> But sweeter far Thy face to see,
>   And in Thy presence rest.
>
> No voice can sing, nor heart can frame,
>   Nor can the memory find
> A sweeter sound than Thy blest Name,
>   O Saviour of mankind!
>
> O Hope of every contrite heart!
>   O Joy of all the meek!
> To those who ask, how kind Thou art!
>   How good to those who seek!
>
> But what to those who find? ah! this
>   No tongue nor pen can show:
> The love of Jesus, what it is,
>   None but His loved ones know.
>
> Jesus, our only joy be Thou,
>   As Thou our prize wilt be;
> In Thee be all our glory now,
>   And through eternity.
>
> —*Bernard of Clairvaux*

* * *

UNDER TO

MY LITTLE two-year-old son had been learning Bible verses, which he recited at the time of family prayer each day. One morning he essayed Luke 18:16, which he quoted in this fashion: "Suffer the little children to come *under* to me." That is not an accurate quotation, but as a reflection of the spirit and manner in which one must come to Christ it is very accurate indeed. Not only a little child but also the man or the woman who comes to Christ comes *under* to Him. The man who is saved placed himself under the blood which Christ shed for man's redemption. Surrender to the Lord Jesus means coming under His dominion, bringing oneself under allegiance to Him. The surrendered believer takes upon himself the yoke of Christ and bows his shoulders under His burden. The Lord tells us His yoke is easy and His burden is light, but no yoke can be placed on a neck that is not bowed and no burden can be carried on a back unbent.

No man can be saved until he recognizes himself as a sinner and is conscious of his need of salvation. The proud of heart and the haughty of spirit must be humbled and brought low if he is to experience the saving grace of God. It is by simple, trusting faith in the Lord Jesus Christ that men are redeemed. "Except ye be converted, and become as little children," says Christ, "ye shall not enter into the kingdom of heaven." Trusting Christ, we serve under His leadership; we fight under His banner; we rest under His love; we trust under His power. Our sins are under His blood; our lives are under His care; our wills are under His command. Coming to Christ, we come out from under the guilt of sins, from under the wrath of God, which abides on the unbeliever (John 3:36). When we come to Christ it is a coming "under to" Him. Our wills, our lives, our thoughts, and our duties are brought into captivity to the Lord Jesus. We are subjects under His sway, whom we acknowledge as the King of our lives.

I am coming to the cross;
    I am poor and weak and blind;
I am counting all but dross:
    I shall full salvation find.

Here I give my all to Thee,
　Friends and time and earthly store;
Soul and body Thine to be,
　Wholly Thine forevermore.

Gladly I accept Thy grace;
　Gladly I obey Thy Word;
All Thy promises embrace,
　O my Saviour and my Lord.

I am trusting, Lord, in Thee,
　Blessed Lamb of Calvary;
Humbly at Thy cross I bow,
　Seeking Thy salvation now.

—William McDonald

* * *

I DO NOT KNOW

THERE is much I do not know; there is much I cannot know.

I do not know what a day may bring forth. I do not know what tomorrow has in store for me. I do not know what will be the outcome of the things I undertake.

I do not know where the path of life may lead me before I reach its end. I do not know where sorrow awaits along the way or where death lurks. I do not know where I may come across something which I would like to escape.

I do not know when I may be afflicted with sickness or disease. I do not know when I may be called upon to pass through a fiery trial or when tragedy may strike. I do not know when a loved one may be taken away or when I shall be called to join those who have gone before.

I do not know why sorrows come into our lives. I do not know why innocent people are called upon to suffer for the sins of others. I do not know why things which I desire are denied me nor why things which I would avoid are thrust upon me.

I do not know how the flesh can stand the suffering which

it is sometimes called upon to endure. I do not know how the soul can go through the waters deep and chill, which threaten to engulf it. I do not know how to reconcile God's love for men with the terrible tragedy and suffering which Divine Providence visits upon them.

But, I do not need to know what, nor when, nor how, nor why, because I do know "whom I have believed" (II Timothy 1:12). I know God. In the Lord Jesus Christ I find Him perfectly revealed. The God I know is a God of love. His love is manifest in the death of Christ on the cross for our sins. He loved us and gave Himself for us. The God I know is wise. He is the Author of all wisdom and all knowledge. He knows the end from the beginning. The God I know is omnipotent. He upholds "all things by the word of his power."

I can trust Him who is Himself perfect love and power and wisdom. He knows what I need and understands what is best for me, and He will not permit anything else to come into my life. He is able to give me strength to face whatever may come into my life.

Do you know Him?

> I heard the voice of Jesus say,
>   "Come unto Me and rest;
> Lay down, thou weary one, lay down
>   Thy head upon My breast."
> I came to Jesus as I was,
>   Weary and worn and sad;
> I found in Him a resting place,
>   And He has made me glad.
>
> I heard the voice of Jesus say,
>   "Behold, I freely give
> The living water; thirsty one,
>   Stoop down and drink, and live!"
> I came to Jesus, and I drank
>   Of that life-giving stream;
> My thirst was quenched, my soul revived,
>   And now I live in Him.

I heard the voice of Jesus say,
"I am this dark world's light;
Look unto Me; thy morn shall rise,
And all thy day be bright!"
I looked to Jesus, and I found
In Him my star, my sun;
And in that light of life I'll walk,
Till traveling days are done.

—*Horatius Bonar*

* * *

HE KNOWS HIS OWN

IN Westminster Abbey on the tomb of Britain's "unknown soldier" of the First World War is carved a portion of II Timothy 2:19: "The Lord knoweth them that are his."

The Bible teaches that a sinner lost and undone, without hope here and hereafter, by simple faith in the Lord Jesus Christ as his personal Saviour becomes a child of God, a member of the family of God. Just as a father knows the names of his children, so the Lord knows the names of those who belong to Him. As a shepherd can identify his sheep though they may be mixed with a strange flock, so the Divine Shepherd identifies the sheep of His flock wherever they may be among the kindreds and tribes and nations of the world.

This verse brings great comfort to God's people in times of trial. When war strikes, families are separated, sons go off to battle, homes are broken by the invader and parents lose contact with children, but in the midst of all the turmoil and chaos and confusion, the Lord still knows His own. To whatever spot they may have been removed His eye has followed them. In a world that has been cursed with war upon war, amid the destruction of armies, God's eye has seen as His own have fallen on the field of battle. Amid the carnage on the seas He has watched as His children have gone down to death in the deep waters. He has watched

planes speeding through the flaming air and has seen the
fall of His own to the earth.

Just as the Lord called His friend Lazarus by name, bidding
him come forth from the grave, so on some glorious day
the dead in Christ shall rise at the sound of His voice speaking to His own, "Come forth!" God's family will some day
be united; but now scattered over the earth He knows them
that are His, and He keeps watch also even above the
scattered dust of His sleeping children. The Lord knows
them that are His and in all the darkness of bloody days
"standeth God within the shadows keeping watch above His
own."

> Lord, it belongs not to my care
>   Whether I die or live;
> To love and serve Thee is my share,
>   And this Thy grace must give.
>
> If life be long, I will be glad,
>   That I may long obey;
> If short, yet why should I be sad
>   To soar to endless day?
>
> Christ leads me through no darker rooms
>   Than He went through before;
> He that into God's kingdom comes
>   Must enter by this door.
>
> Come, Lord, when grace has made me meet
>   Thy blessed face to see:
> For if Thy work on earth be sweet,
>   What will Thy glory be!
>
> My knowledge of that life is small,
>   The eye of faith is dim;
> But 'tis enough that Christ knows all,
>   And I shall be with Him.
>   —*Richard Baxter*

*   *   *

GOD'S MEMORY

GOD manifests His grace and goodness in the things which
He remembers. A man whose life has been sinful and vile,

who has on his soul the guilt and weight of all kinds of
sin, trusts Christ as his Saviour and his guilt is washed away
in the blood of the cross. God says to the poor sinner who
has been saved by grace concerning his sins that He will
remember them against him no more forever. Not only is
the guilt washed away, not only is the burden lifted, not
only are the sins forgiven—as far as God is concerned, they
are *forgotten* as well.

This is what God forgets for the one who by faith in
Christ becomes a child of God: the deeds of his sinful past.
But the God who is so merciful in His forgetting is gracious
in His remembering, too, for He never fails to keep a record
of the good deeds and kind words of His children. He remembers them to reward them. Even the giving of a cup of
cold water in His Name He does not forget.

The book of Malachi tells us that "they that feared the
Lord spake often one to another: and the Lord hearkened,
and heard it, and a book of remembrance was written before
him" (Malachi 3:16). The God of the universe sets down
in the record the kind things which people who love Him say
about Him. One day those who have been saved by grace
through faith will stand before Him, not to be judged for
the sins they committed before they were saved, for God
has completely forgotten them, but they will stand before
Him to receive a reward and He in that hour will recall
to mind all that they have done and said for love of Him.
Not one word will be forgotten, not one deed will be un-
remembered, but each shall have its reward.

> "But gather all My saints," He cries,
> "That made their peace with God,
> By the Redeemer's sacrifice,
> And seal'd it with His blood.
>
> Their faith and works brought forth to light
> Shall make the world confess
> My sentence of reward is right,
> And heaven adore My grace."
>   —*Isaac Watts*

SECRETS SHARED

GOD came to visit Abraham and Abraham was host to God Himself. This occasion is described in the eighteenth chapter of Genesis. In the likeness of man, the Lord and two angelic companions appeared to Abraham one day as he sat in the door of his tent. The hospitable patriot made them rest themselves in the shade while he washed their feet and set food before them. After the visit, Abraham went with them to bring them on their way toward Sodom. As the two angels went on toward the condemned city, the Lord Himself lingered behind to talk over His plans with his friend Abraham, saying, "Shall I hide from Abraham that thing which I do?" (Genesis 18:17).

What a wonderful privilege to entertain the Lord! What a glorious experience to share with Him the secrets of His omniscient mind. Yet, while we envy Abraham the intimacy and fellowship of this occasion, we forget that it is a privilege which we may enjoy. "Behold, I stand at the door, and knock: if any man hear my voice, and open the door, I will come in to him, and will sup with him, and he with me" (Revelation 3:20). The Lord still tells His friends the things which He is going to do. In the Word He still declares to us not only His plans for the world but also the things which He is preparing for those who love Him. Christ says to us, "I go to prepare a place for you. And if I go and prepare a place for you, I will come again, and receive you unto myself; that where I am, there ye may be also" (John 14:2, 3). He reveals the judgments and the destruction which He will pour out on this world of iniquity and sin as He revealed to Abraham that His wrath was to be poured out in fire upon Sodom and Gomorrah.

God would not have His child ignorant of His plans. He wants us to know that the dead shall be raised again, that the throne of the Lord shall be established in this earth, that every knee shall bow, and every tongue shall confess that

Christ is Lord to the glory of God the Father, that when He shall reign the redeemed shall reign with Him. As much as our finite minds can comprehend of His divine purpose and plans, He tells us and for our joy assures us that beyond all we can comprehend, "Eye hath not seen, nor ear heard, neither have entered into the heart of man, the things which God hath prepared for them that love him" (I Corinthians 2:9).

Nor eye has seen, nor ear has heard,
Nor sense nor reason known
What joys the Father has prepar'd
For those that love the Son.

But the good Spirit of the Lord
Reveals a heaven to come:
The beams of glory in His Word
Allure and guide us home.

Those holy gates forever bar
Pollution, sin and shame;
None shall obtain admittance there
But followers of the Lamb.

He keeps the Father's book of life,
There all their names are found;
The hypocrite in vain shall strive
To tread the heavenly ground.

—*Isaac Watts*

* * *

REPAYMENT IN ACCEPTANCE

It is impossible for any man to repay God for His goodness. Man has no gifts to offer God but those with which God has endowed him. Everything in the universe belongs to the God who made all things. The wealth of mines, expanse of fertile fields, all that makes a man rich, supports life, or delight the eye comes as a gift from the Creator. "He maketh his sun to rise on the evil and on the good, and sendeth rain on the just and on the unjust" (Matthew

5:45). He "giveth to all men liberally" (James 1:5). Man has nothing to offer God since all belongs to God anyway and has merely been poured out on man from the bountiful hand of a loving Creator.

The psalmist, feeling the impossibility of requiting God for His goodness, cries out, "What shall I render unto the Lord for all his benefits toward me?" (Psalm 116:12). Then he answers his question in these words: "I will take the cup of salvation, and call upon the name of the Lord" (verse 13). Man cannot repay God for His goodness. The only offering which he can make in return is one of thankful acceptance. To accept the gift with a heart full of praise and love for the Giver is the only way that man can in any degree recompense God. God gives because He loves. Thankful acceptance springing from a heart of love is the only return Deity desires for His gifts.

The greatest of all God's gifts is the gift of His Son. Accepting Him as Saviour, the thankful heart of a redeemed sinner takes the cup of salvation. Hard of heart and thoughtless and inconsiderate is the man who accepts God's gifts without calling upon His Name in thanksgiving. Hard of heart indeed is the man who despises God's love and rejects His greatest gift—Jesus Christ.

> I sought the Lord, and afterward I knew
> He moved my soul to seek Him, seeking me;
> It was not I that found, O Saviour true;
> No, I was found of Thee.
>
> Thou didst reach forth Thy hand and mine enfold;
> I walked and sank not on the storm-vexed sea,
> 'Twas not so much that I on Thee took hold,
> As Thou, dear Lord, on me.
>
> I find, I walk, I love, but, O the whole
> Of love is but my answer, Lord, to Thee!
> For Thou wert long beforehand with my soul;
> Always Thou lovedst me.
>
> —*Anonymous*

"Search Me, O God"

Psalm 139:23

GHOSTS DO NOT WALK

Twice the disciples thought Jesus Christ was a ghost. The first time they were in a storm on the sea and they beheld Him walking on the water (Matthew 14:25, 26). The second time the disciples, still unconvinced of His resurrection, were gathered in the upper room where He suddenly appeared in their midst (Luke 24:36, 37).

What a strange and stupid thing that the disciples should twice take refuge from the miraculous in the superstitious, supposing they beheld a ghost rather than accepting the manifest evidence of their own eyes — that He Himself stood before them!

How much more logical on the first occasion to believe that the One who made the water should use it for a highway! How much more reasonable the second time to accept the evidence of His physical presence in the wound prints in hands and feet and side!

At the root of this strange and stupid attitude was lack of faith and hesitancy to accept that which was, from the standpoint of human reasoning, impossible. Having seen Christ perform many miracles, they should have accepted these miraculous manifestations of His power over natural law and over death without surprise, but such was not the case.

Christ said, "All power is given unto me in heaven and in earth." This is nothing impossible for omnipotent Deity. The man who recognizes an omnipotent God has no trouble believing in the miraculous. When our minds limit Deity, naturally our hearts will lack faith. Men question the historical accuracy and the inspiration of the Bible because it recounts miraculous happenings which they are unwilling to accept. Grant that God is able to do all things and there is no room for doubts as to the authority and accuracy of His Word. Men accept the foolish and impossible evolutionary theory of the creation of life because they limit God. They refuse to recognize a Deity who by the Word of His omnipotence created the universe and made man in His own image. Because men limit God's power they, like the disciples, saying, "It is a spirit," believe a theory full of obvious errors and manifest impossibilities rather than accept the Genesis statement of simple truth having Divine Omnipotence as its foundation. The God who made the universe, who hung the world on nothing and the North on the empty space, is certainly able to perform the miracles recorded in the book of Jonah. The God who created all material things could certainly turn water into wine and feed five thousand men with five loaves and two fishes.

> Behold the blind their sight receive;
> Behold the dead awake and live;
> The dumb speak wonders, and the lame
> Leap like the hart, and bless His Name.
>
> Thus doth th' eternal Spirit own
> And seal the mission of the Son;
> The Father vindicates His cause
> While He hangs bleeding on the cross.
>
> He dies; the heavens in mourning stood;
> He rises, and appears a God;
> Behold the Lord ascending high,
> No more to bleed, no more to die.
>
> Hence and forever from my heart
> I bid my doubts and fears depart,
> And to Those hands my soul resign
> Which bear credentials so divine.
>
> —*Isaac Watts*

* * *

ASKING FOR A RAISE

SOMETIMES as we study the life of the Saviour we overlook the sorrows which His friends must have caused Him. The disciples were so slow to understand the truths He sought to teach them. They were greedy for preferment and place. They were such poor representatives of His perfection and love. They protested so much and did so little. In the hour of His betrayal and suffering they forsook Him or followed afar off.

One of the saddest examples of the disciples' lack of sympathy and understanding of the Saviour is recorded in the tenth chapter of Mark (verses 32-45). There we are told, "He took again the twelve, and began to tell them what things should happen unto him." He wanted them to understand that in Jerusalem, to which they were now going, He would be delivered unto His enemies, condemned to death, crucified. Just as Christ finished describing the anguish and sorrow which lay ahead of Him, James and John spoke up asking for the positions of highest importance and greatest glory in His kingdom. These two disciples had their minds so occupied with their own greedy ambitions that they seem not to have heard at all the words of the Lord. In the very moment when He was describing the suffering which He must endure they were asking for honor and glory.

With this attitude of heart and with minds so preoccupied, it is no wonder that the disciples failed to understand the truths Christ spoke concerning Himself and His redemptive work. It is no wonder that the death of Christ on the cross left them feeling that everything was at an end. It is no wonder that the resurrection seemed to take them by surprise. They listened so halfheartedly, so absent-mindedly to the words of the Saviour as He showed them the suffering and the cross and the open tomb which lay ahead. Their minds were on the kingdom and power for themselves. Their selfish dreams and ambitions shut from their consciousness the necessity of the cross. Even Peter, who seems at least to have listened when the Lord foretold His death, cried out, "Be it far from thee, Lord" (Matthew 16:22). The disciples had not learned the lesson that suffering must come before glory and that through the low gateway of anguish and death leads the path to a throne.

> O for a heart to praise my God,
>   A heart from sin set free,
> A heart that always feels Thy blood
>   So freely spilt for me!
>
> A heart resigned, submissive, meek,
>   My great Redeemer's throne;
> Where only Christ is heard to speak,
>   Where Jesus reigns alone;
>
> A humble, lowly, contrite heart,
>   Believing, true, and clean,
> Which neither life nor death can part
>   From Him that dwells within;
>
> A heart in every thought renewed,
>   And full of love divine;
> Perfect, and right, and pure, and good,
>   A copy, Lord, of Thine!
>
> Thy nature, gracious Lord, impart;
>   Come quickly from above;
> Write Thy new name upon my heart,
>   Thy new, best name of love.
>   —*Charles Wesley*

* * *

THE PARALYSIS OF FEAR

FEAR! How it grips the human heart! How it paralyzes with cold terror! But for the Christian it is an emotion that never need be felt. "For God hath not given us the spirit of fear; but of power, and of love, and of a sound mind" (II Timothy 1:7).

Fear and a sound mind are not found together. Fear makes a man act with unreasoning instinct, not with the logical accuracy of sound thought. Possessed by it, the mind cannot function accurately and clearly. But love and a sound mind are a natural combination. Love stimulates life. Love motivates action and thought along the highest planes. Pure love can move men to the finest of creative effort and artistic endeavor and tireless activity.

Fear can become man's greatest enemy. Shakespeare said, "Cowards die many times before their deaths. But the valiant never taste of death but once." Love is an ally that never knows defeat. Even death itself holds no terrors when love is by one's side.

The child of God is called to the "spirit of love," and he who lives up to that high calling is freed from the bondage of fear for "perfect love casteth out fear" (I John 4:18).

If we have experienced the love of God fully there is no room left in the heart for fear. "God is love" (I John 4:8), and resting in Him all is calm and confidence. However alarming external conditions may be, however dreadful may appear the circumstances with which one is surrounded, the Christian trusts unafraid in the love of God.

That God loves us is evident. "For God so loved the world, that he gave his only begotten Son, that whosoever believeth in him should not perish, but have everlasting life" (John 3:16). A God who loves so greatly is not a God who will permit anything to come into the life of His child except what is best for him. An all-wise God surely is a competent judge of what is best! As a child trusts the love of his mother and leaves the problems of his little life to her solution, so may the Christian trust his life to the keeping of a loving God.

We may not understand God's choices for us now. We may not know why He permits some things to cross our paths. We may not comprehend His perfect will when the clouds hide the sun and the smoke of war darkens our sky. But with "a sound mind" and perfect confidence, God's child rests in "the love of Christ, which passeth knowledge" (Ephesians 3:19).

> Child of My love, fear not the unknown morrow,
>   Dread not the new demand life makes of thee;
> Thy ignorance doth hold no cause for sorrow
>   Since what thou knowest not is known to Me.
>
> Thou canst not see today the hidden meaning
>   Of My command, but thou the light shalt gain;
> Walk on in faith, upon My promise leaning,
>   And as Thou goest all shall be made plain,
>
> One step thou seest—then go forward boldly,
>   One step is far enough for faith to see;
> Take that, and thy next duty shall be told thee,
>   For step by step thy Lord is leading thee.
>
> Stand not in fear thy adversaries counting,
>   Dare every peril, save to disobey;
> Thou shalt march on, all obstacles surmounting;
>   For I, the Strong, will open up the way.
>
> Wherefore go gladly to the task assigned thee,
>   Having My promise, needing nothing more
> Than just to know, where'er the future find thee,
>   In all thy journeying I go before.
>
> —*Selected*

* * *

A GOOD DEED FOR THE DAY

A MAN who commits a wrong act—who lies, or steals, or murders—is guilty of sin. There is another kind of sin, however, which most of us commit and of which we are rarely conscious. This is not the sin of doing something wrong, but the sin of failing to do something which is right—the sin of omission. Some sins are not things we do. Some sins are things we "don't"! Such sin often springs from carelessness, selfishness or indifference, and the child of God is as frequently guilty of this kind of sin as is the unconverted man. We have an opportunity to say a word which will bring comfort into a heart heavy with grief and we fail to take advantage of the opportunity. We fail to take the time to help another who is burdened and perplexed. We fail to be generous to those who are in need. Oftentimes we fail in these things because we are self-centered and unconcerned and fail to notice the need.

The Bible says, "To him that knoweth to do good, and doeth it not, to him it is sin" (James 4:17). We do wrong often, but we fail to do right more often! Those are guilty of the sin of omission to whom the King when He comes in His glory shall say, "For I was an hungred, and ye gave me no meat . . . naked, and ye clothed me not: sick, and in prison, and ye visited me not. Then shall they also answer him, saying, Lord, when saw we thee an hungred, or athirst, or a stranger, or naked, or sick, or in prison, and did not minister unto thee? Then shall he answer them, saying, Verily I say unto you, Inasmuch as ye did it not to one of the least of these, ye did it not to me" (Matthew 25:42-45). The Word does not record their having added to the load or increased the burden of those in sickness and in sorrow and in prison. Their sin was the sin of failing to lift the load and ease the burden. There are very few of us who do not need to pray with honest hearts, "We have left undone those things which we ought to have done; and we have done those things which we ought not to have done. And there is no health in us."

> The bread that bringeth strength I want to give,
> The water pure that bids the thirsty live;
> I want to help the fainting day by day;
> I'm sure I shall not pass again this way.
>
> I want to give the oil of joy for tears,
> The faith to conquer crowding doubts and fears,
> Beauty for ashes may I give away,
> I'm sure I shall not pass again this way.

I want to give good measure running o'er,
And into hungry hearts I want to pour
The answer soft that turneth wrath away;
I'm sure I shall not pass again this way.

I want to give to others hope and faith,
I want to do all that the Master saith;
I want to live aright from day to day,
I'm sure I shall not pass again this way.

—*W. R. Fitch*

* * *

THE WHITE FLAG

DISCOURAGEMENT is the great enemy of achievement. We start out with much enthusiasm and when we do not immediately see the results or if the obstacles are greater than we anticipated, the temptation is to say, "Well, I cannot do it anyway," and give up. Most of us are tempted by discouragement to quit. Oftentimes the difference between the man who is a failure and the man who is a success is that one yields to the temptation and the other resists it. This holds not only in the struggle for material things, for fame and knowledge, but also in the struggle to live a victorious Christian life. We grow weary in welldoing.

It was discouragement which caused Elijah under the juniper tree to pray for death. "It is enough," he said, referring to the opposition of the rulers of Israel to his message and the power of the priests of Baal and the hardness of heart of the people. "It is enough," he said, meaning, "I have had all I can stand. I cannot take any more." Any man who tries to accomplish anything for God in the world feels like making the prophet's wail a duet by blending his cry with the discouraged Elijah's "It is enough." This is the cry of a weary body and a tired mind and a heavy heart. It is the cry of the man who has given up the struggle with the goal unachieved or who is despondent because of the difficulties and trials that harass him. It is the cry of surrender, of defeat and failure.

But there is another cry of victory and fulfillment, the peal of triumph when the job is done. This is the cry of the Lord on the cross when He saw man's redemption accomplished and the price of sin paid. "It is finished" (John 19:30). This is no languid sigh. It is a shout of triumph. What an example of perseverance to the end we find in this and the circumstances which went before it! "He stedfastly set his face to go to Jerusalem" (Luke 9:51) to die. "As a sheep before her shearers is dumb, so he openeth not his mouth" (Isaiah 53:7) beneath the blows of the lash, the jeers and the persecution and the piercing of the thorny crown. He never hesitated. He "endured the cross, despising the shame" (Hebrews 12:2). There is no word of complaint, but at the end the shout of victory. How much better the cry, "It is finished," when the task is completed, than the sigh, "It is enough," when the work is only half done.

" 'Tis finished!" so the Saviour cried,
    And meekly bowed His head and died;
'Tis finished! yes, the race is run,
    The battle fought, the victory won.

'Tis finished! all that heaven foretold
    By prophets in the days of old,
And truths are opened to our view
    That kings and prophets never knew.

'Tis finished! Son of God, Thy power
    Hath triumphed in this awful hour,
And yet our eyes with sorrow see
    That life to us was death to Thee.

'Tis finished! let the joyful sound
    Be heard through all the nations round;
'Tis finished! let the triumph rise
    And swell the chorus of the skies!

    —*Samuel Stennett*

WORDS WITHOUT KNOWLEDGE

THERE are many wonderful lessons for us in the book of Job. It is great drama and great literature. As one of the books in the inspired Word of God it is a source of truth and blessing, but in this modern day its riches are often left unexplored.

Job was a prosperous man who honored God. Satan charged that he served the Lord because it paid him. God, to prove Job's faithfulness, granted Satan permission to afflict him. His children were killed; his property was swept away; he was afflicted with a loathsome disease. Friends came to commiserate with him, but their conversation was a source of irritation to Job and their "comfort" mocked him. They professed great wisdom about spiritual matters and great understanding of the way in which God worked, but their philosophy was full of falsehood and their arguments stupid and ill conceived as they attempted to convince Job that he suffered because he had committed some secret sin. "Who ever perished, being innocent? or where were the righteous cut off?" (Job 4:7), they asked, and even Job himself was convinced that God had not dealt justly with him.

Finally, God's voice sounded from the whirlwind, "Who is this that darkeneth counsel by words without knowledge?" (Job 38:2). The conceit of man in questioning the wisdom of God was challenged with the question, "Where wast thou when I laid the foundations of the earth?" (Job 38:4).

How well might these two questions be addressed to some in our twentieth century who are full of opinions without knowledge. The very air is blue with the empty words of self-important men. Listening to them talk, one would think they knew better than Almighty God how to run the world. They offer advice about problems of which they have no comprehension. They darken counsel "by words without knowledge."

Hearing people, even Christian people, question the goodness and wisdom of God in His dealings with them and with the world which He has made, one cannot help wishing that the Voice out of the whirlwind would ask again, "Where wast thou when I laid the foundations of the earth?"

> O Thou Eternal One! whose presence bright
> All space doth occupy, all motions guide;
> Unchanged through time's all-devastating flight;
> Thou only God! There is no God beside!
> Being of all beings! Mighty One!
> Whom none could comprehend and none explore;
> Who fillest existence with Thyself alone:
> Embracing all, supporting, ruling o'er—
> Being whom we call God, and know no more!
>
> In its sublime research, philosophy
> May measure out the ocean deeps, may count
> The sands or the sun's rays; but God! for Thee
> There is no weight nor measure: none can mount
> Up to Thy mysteries. Reason's brightest spark,
> Though kindled by Thy light, in vain would try
> To trace Thy counsels, infinite and dark,
> And thought is lost ere thought can soar so high,
> Even like past moments in eternity.
>
> —Derzhavin

* * *

WANTS AND WISHES

"But, Daddy, I need it," said the little boy. He had asked his father for chewing gum. His father had said teasingly, "Why should I give it to you, Jimmie?" Jimmie wanted the gum so much that he thought he needed it.

There are many folk like Jimmie. They confuse their wishes with their needs. Some things it would be nice to have are not at all necessary. Things we think essential to our life and happiness we discover we can do very well without.

God has promised His children that He will supply their needs. The Bible says to the Christian, "My God shall supply all your need according to his riches in glory by Christ Jesus" (Philippians 4:19). But that is not enough for some of us. We wish to see our wants supplied also, and we feel that God neglects or forgets us when He does not give us exactly what we want when we want it. We have enough to eat, and enough to wear, and much more, but we want our own favorite nonessential, too. Like Jimmie, we "need" our chewing gum.

Our lives would be much happier if we would trust our Heavenly Father to give what is best and let Him decide what things we need. His judgment in such matters is better than ours. Jesus Christ said, "Your Father knoweth what things ye have need of" (Matthew 6:8). This does not only include temporal things like food and clothes. It covers also our spiritual need, the need of strength in the time of temptation, of comfort in the time of sorrow, of inner peace in the time of war. As God's child you may not only have the great joy of trusting your Father with the assurance in your heart that He will supply your needs, but you may also enjoy freedom from the responsibility of deciding what the needs are. All needs are met in Jesus Christ. Only He is able to save from sin and every man needs salvation. In Him are also wisdom and knowledge and power. Having Him, we have all needful things beside. "But seek ye first the kingdom of God, and his righteousness; and all these things shall be added unto you" (Matthew 6:33).

THE BLIND CHILD

I know what Mother's face is like,
    Although I cannot see;
It's like the music of a bell;
It's like the roses I can smell—
    Yes, these it's like to me.

I know what Father's face is like;
  I'm sure I know it all;
It's like his whistle on the air;
It's like his arms which take such care
  And never let me fall.

And I can tell what God is like—
  The God whom no one sees.
He's everything my parents seem;
He's fairer than my fondest dream,
  And greater than all these.

                                    —*Anonymous*

* * *

GUILTY

ONE of the most common faults of the human race is
the fault of self-deception. We cannot seem to see ourselves
as we really are. It is easy to see the fault in the other man,
but it is extremely difficult to discover and acknowledge our
own. That our neighbor has a vile temper we are quick to
admit. We are reluctant to confess our own. In him it is
"temper." In us it is "righteous indignation." A business
associate of ours we consider dishonest, but when our own
dealings are a little "'shady," that is simply a "smart move"
or a "clever policy." It is easy to hear the preacher's words
and think how they apply to Brother So-and-So and fail to
consider that they apply even more to us.

The Prophet Nathan came to King David and told him
that there was a certain man in his kingdom who had many
sheep and who wanted to prepare a banquet, but instead of
slaughtering one of his own flock he stole the one pet lamb
which his neighbor owned and killed that and served it.
David, full of indignation and wrath at so cruel and so
wicked a man, cried out, "As the Lord liveth, the man that
hath done this thing shall surely die: and he shall restore
the lamb fourfold, because he did this thing and because

he had no pity" (II Samuel 12:5, 6). The prophet pointed
a stern finger at the king and cried, "Thou art the man"
(verse 7), and the prophet proceeded to uncover the meaning
of the parable of the man who killed his neighbor's sheep.
David, the king, had taken advantage of his royal power
to rob another man of his wife and to send him to the front
line of battle to be slain. David was indignant over a sheep
stolen by another, but had been completely unconcerned about
his own great sin. Having been so dramatically reminded of
his guilt, he repented and prayed for forgiveness.

Which of us does not need to pray, "Search me, O God,
and know my heart: try me, and know my thoughts (Psalm
139:23).

> Sin has a thousand treacherous arts
>   To practice on the mind;
> With flattering looks she tempts our hearts,
>   But leaves a sting behind.
>
> With names of virtue she deceives
>   The aged and the young;
> And while the heedless wretch believes,
>   She makes his fetters strong.
>
> She pleads for all the joys she brings,
>   And gives a fair pretence;
> But cheats the soul of heavenly things,
>   And chains it down to sense.
>
> —Isaac Watts

* * *

NO REASON FOR FEAR

THE Bible tells of many people who were afraid when
there was no reason for fear. We are told that when Peter
and James and John beheld the transfiguration of the Lord
Jesus, "they were sore afraid" (Mark 9:6). The glory of
His face and the appearance of Moses and Elias by His side

frightened them so much that they did not know what to say, and the thrill of a great experience brought terror to their hearts.

The disciples were caught in a storm at sea and they were so afraid that they woke Jesus, saying, "Master, carest thou not that we perish?" (Mark 4:38). How could they fear that the boat in which the God of the sea was riding would be swallowed by the sea!

A woman who had been ill for years and had been unable to find a physician to cure her, touched the hem of Christ's garment as He passed down crowded streets one day and when He turned and asked, "Who touched me?" (Mark 5:31), she fell down "fearing and trembling" before Him. Surely, this woman whose faith in God's Son was so great that she was healed by the touch of His garment had no reason to fear Him who came into the world to give men life.

The women came to the tomb of Christ. They found the stone rolled away, the Lord risen, and an angel on guard, and "they were affrighted" (Mark 16:5). Here was no cause for fear. The angel was there to give them the glorious message that Christ was risen.

Christian people today all too often are fearful when there is nothing of which to be afraid. The future should hold no terror for God's child. The power of God should not frighten those who know His love. The storms of this world should not terrify those of whose lives Christ is the pilot. Men who are out of Christ have much to fear. They are lost here and hereafter, but God's child in daily fellowship with the Saviour should hear Him say, "It is I, be not afraid" (Matthew 14:27).

> Give to the winds thy fears;
>   Hope and be undismayed;
> God hears thy sighs and counts thy tears,
>   God shall lift up thy head.

Through waves and clouds and storms
   He gently clears thy way;
Wait thou His time; so shall this night
   Soon end in joyous day.

Leave to His sovereign sway
   To choose and to command;
So shalt thou, wondering, own His way,
   How wise, how strong His hand!

Far, far above thy thought
   His counsel shall appear,
When fully He the work hath wrought
   That caused thy needless fear.

—*Paul Gerhardt*

*   *   *

FOLLOW THE LEADER

IT SOMETIMES seems to me that the worst sin of our day
is the sin of conformity. We fall in line too readily. What
other people do, we do. All too often those who claim
to be Christians imitate in their lives and habits those who
do not claim to be Christians. Many a man violates his conscience rather than be thought peculiar by refusing to do
something he knows is wrong. There is many a young woman
who accepts a cocktail because friends around her drink them,
and because in the set in which she moves it has become
an accepted custom.

We need nonconformists. "Be not conformed to this
world: but be ye transformed by the renewing of your mind,
that ye may prove what is that good, and acceptable, and
perfect, will of God" (Romans 12:2) is a good motto for
Christian people in our day. They are not supposed to follow
with blind devotion the popular practice, but be directed
by God's will. That which is intrinsically wrong does not
become right because it becomes commonplace. Sin is sin
whether it is popular or not. The great souls who have
blessed the world have not been those who went with the

crowd. They have been those who went *against* the crowd. Many of them were willing to die to be different. They gave their lives for holding to an ideal or a truth counter to the practices and beliefs of their day. Today many people would rather die than be different.

When God gave Moses instructions for His chosen people, He included this admonition: "Thou shalt not follow a multitude to do evil" (Exodus 23:2). The tendency of the multitude is away from God and along the pathway of selfish gratification. He who follows the multitude is apt to find himself more often than not doing evil.

> Come, Saviour, Jesus from above!
>   Assist me with Thy heavenly grace,
> Empty my heart of earthly love,
>   And for Thyself prepare the place.
>
> O let Thy sacred presence fill,
>   And set my longing spirit free!
> Which pants to have no other will,
>   But day and night to feast on Thee.
>
> While in this region here below,
>   No other good will I pursue:
> I'll bid this world of noise and show,
>   With all its glittering snares, adieu!
>
> That path with humble speed I'll seek,
>   In which my Saviour's footsteps shine;
> Nor will I hear, nor will I speak,
>   Of any other love but Thine.
>
> Henceforth may no profane delight
>   Divide this consecrated soul;
> Possess it, Thou who hast the right,
>   As Lord and Master of the whole.
>
> —*Antoinette Bourignon*

* * *

THE MINORITY WITH GOD

MANY phrases glibly quoted as popular sayings are far from true. Such a phrase is: "The majority is always right." As a matter of fact, it is to be questioned whether the majority is not more often wrong than right. There certainly can be no doubt that the majority is often wrong.

In the days of Copernicus the majority believed that the earth was the center of the universe. In the time of Columbus the majority believed that the world was flat.

Truth is often nurtured and protected by the minority against the attacks and assaults of the majority. Majorities have sent martyrs to the stake. Majorities have crushed liberty and exalted false political theories. The great men and women of the world—those who have been pioneers of progress and enlightenment—have belonged to minorities. All too often the minority has called attention to a truth by suffering for it at the hands of the majority.

Jesus Christ said, "Wide is the gate, and broad is the way, that leadeth to destruction, and many there be which go in thereat: because strait is the gate, and narrow is the way, which leadeth unto life, and few there be that find it" (Matthew 7:13, 14). How true His Word is, has been proved by the conduct of men down the centuries. It is being proved today. The majority are greedy for gain, seeking their own pleasure, choosing their own way. The enjoyment of each passing moment and the accumulation of possessions are their chief purposes in life. How few in comparison choose the way of Christ, who said, "If any man will come after me, let him deny himself, and take up his cross, and follow me" (Matthew 16:24). How few choose the things which belong to eternity and not to time!

No, the majority is not always right. The majority usually follows unthinkingly the line of least resistance and greatest immediate personal gratification. The majority is not concerned with truth. The majority seeks what is popular.

Christ's minority walks an unpopular way. They go like lambs among wolves. They are not concerned with being up-to-date and popular. They are, as far as this world is concerned, a minority, but it is better to be in the minority with God than in the majority without Him.

My Redeemer and my Lord,
I beseech Thee, I entreat Thee,
Guide me in each act and word,
That hereafter I may meet Thee,
Watching, waiting, hoping, yearning,
With my lamp well trimmed and burning,
Interceding with these bleeding wounds
   Upon Thy hands and side,
For all who have lived and erred,
   Thou hast suffered,
   Thou hast died,
Scourged and mocked and crucified,
And in the grave hast Thou been buried.

If my feeble prayer can reach Thee,
Oh, my Saviour, I beseech Thee,
Even as Thou hast died for me,
   More sincerely
Let me follow where Thou leadest,
Let me, bleeding as Thou bleedest,
Die if dying I may give
Life to one who asks to live,
   And more nearly,
Dying thus, resemble Thee.

—Henry Wadsworth Longfellow

*   *   *

THE POINT OF VIEW

THE angle from which we look at an object is largely responsible for the impression which the object makes upon us. The place where we stand governs our outlook. The "point of view" affects the vision.

God had led the children of Israel out of Egypt. They

were camped on the shore of the Red Sea, closed in by the topography of the land between the water and the army of Pharaoh. The pillar of cloud and fire which had led them by day and by night now settled down between them and the army of Pharaoh like a curtain. To the Egyptians it was "a cloud and darkness." To the Israelites "it gave light by night" (Exodus 14:20). Talk about a cloud with a silver lining! Here is one black and gloomy on one side and a flame of brilliance on the other. The Egyptian army in all the pride of its power had set itself against God's people, and whoever sets himself against them sets himself against God. From their point of view the cloud was darkness. The children of Israel were God's people on God's side, led to this spot by God. No wonder the cloud was all brilliance to them! They were in the right place.

The point of view is important. From the standpoint of time, all our little ambitions, our quest for pleasure and physical satisfaction, seem big and important. From the standpoint of eternity, they are petty and insignificant. Our lives are "as grass."

Men solve one problem after a fashion, and are immediately faced with another more difficult problem. From the purely human standpoint the future at best looks gloomy and foreboding. Seen from the viewpoint of God, the future is bright and glorious. This world is to become the kingdom of our Lord and of His Christ. When God's Son returns to reign, He will solve all problems, settle all strikes.

The Christian should be an optimist. He is in the position always to look on the bright side.

> Long did I toil, and knew no earthly rest,
> Far did I rove, and found no certain home;
> At last I sought them in His sheltering breast,
> Who opes His arms, and bids the weary come:
> With Him I found a home, a rest divine,
> And since then I am His, and He is mine.

The good I have is from His stores supplied,
The ill is only what He deems the best;
He for my Friend, I'm rich with nought beside,
And poor without Him, though of all possessed:
Changes may come—I take, or I resign,
Content, while I am His, while He is mine.
                    —*John Quarles and Henry F. Lyle*

* * *

IT PAYS TO DO RIGHT

AMAZIAH, the king of Judah, was a "practical" man. He hired a hundred thousand mercenary soldiers from Israel, paying them one hundred talents of silver. These men were to join with his own armies in the wars of conquest which he planned, but God was opposed to "the deal." He wanted Judah to be dependent upon Him and not upon hired soldiers. The Lord sent a prophet to Amaziah, who said, "Let not the army of Israel go with thee; for the Lord is not with Israel" (II Chronicles 25:7). Amaziah heard the prophet speak the words of the Lord and then replied, "But what shall we do for the hundred talents which I have given to the army of Israel?" (II Chronicles 25:9). God had spoken. The king's only concern should have been to do that which God commanded, but he was worried about his hundred talents.

There are many people like that today. They know what God wants them to do. They are perfectly aware of what is the right thing to do, but instead of doing it, they weigh the consequences and ask themselves how much it is going to cost them. Business men say, " I know that this is the right thing to do, but I cannot afford to do it. It will hurt my business." Politicians say, "This is the right side of this issue. I should support it, but I cannot afford to. I have to stand in with my constituency. It will cost me votes." There are even some preachers who are unwilling to speak the truth because it may irritate someone who is a prominent member of the church or who helps with his financial support.

Amaziah was not the first man to raise the question about the cost of doing God's will, and he certainly was not the last. The prophet had an answer from God to Amaziah's question, "The Lord is able to give thee much more than this." It is an answer which the man who is tempted to compromise for fear of the cost might take to himself. It "pays" to do right, but men should do right because it is right, even if it does not "pay."

> Almighty and Eternal God, the Disposer of all the affairs of the world, there is not one circumstance so great as not to be subject to Thy power, nor so small but it comes within Thy care; Thy goodness and wisdom show themselves through all Thy works, and Thy loving-kindness and mercy appear in the several dispensations of Thy providence. May we readily submit ourselves to Thy pleasure and sincerely resign our wills to Thine, with all patience, meekness and humility; through Jesus Christ our Lord. Amen.
>
> —*Queen Anne of England*

* * *

MOURN NOT

God does not promise the Christian that he will not have sorrow. The world is full of grief and God's child has no right to expect to be free from it. The Christian as well as the sinner loses his loved ones. He feels the anguish of parting and knows the sadness of death. Indeed, the Christian should not only expect sorrow, he should expect persecution also, for if we would live godly in this present world, we shall suffer persecution (II Timothy 3:12).

But the Christian's sorrow is not like the sorrow of the

sinner. "Ye sorrow not," cried Paul, "even as others which
have no hope" (I Thessalonians 4:13). The sinner sees the
tomb sealed and turns away with no hope of being united
with the loved one laid to rest. To him death is darkness
with no promise of daybreak, night with no hope of dawn.
The Christian beside the tomb of one whom he loves knows
the sorrow of separation but it is "for a little while." The
trusting child of God fallen asleep in Christ has gone to
be with his Lord. Someday his Lord will return. The spirit
of the sleeping Christian will be reunited with his body and
he will come forth from the dust to be caught up with the
living saints in a moment, in the twinkling of an eye (I Corinthians 15:52). Loved ones separated by death will be
reunited for eternity.

The resurrection of the Christian is assured. Christ who
has Himself conquered death, the Risen One who is the
firstfruits of them that sleep, declares, "He that believeth
in me, though he were dead, yet shall he live" (John 11:25).

The Christian can expect sometime to stand under a cloud
of sorrow, but it is a cloud draped with a rainbow of divine
promise of resurrection. We sorrow not as those who have
no hope. Whittier put into poetry his pity for those who
do not have the Christian's blessed hope:

> Alas! for him who never sees
> The stars shine through the cypress-trees!
> Who, hopeless, lays his dead away,
> Nor looks to see the breaking day
> Across the mournful marbles play!
> Who hath not learned, in hours of faith,
> The truth to flesh and sense unknown,
> That Life is ever lord of Death,
> And Love can never lose its own!

O my God! if Thou art pleased to render me a
spectacle to men and angels, Thy holy will be done!
All I ask is that Thou wilt be with and save those
who love Thee, so that neither life nor death, neither
principalities nor powers may ever separate them from

the love of God which is in Jesus Christ. As for me, what matters it what men think of me, or what they make me suffer, since they cannot separate me from that Saviour whose Name is engraven in the very bottom of my heart? If I can only be accepted of Him, I am willing that all men should despise and hate me. Their strokes will polish what may be defective in me, so that I may be presented in peace to Him, for whom I die daily. Without His favor I am wretched. O Saviour! I present myself before Thee an offering, a sacrifice. Purify me in Thy blood, that I may be accepted of Thee. Amen.

—Jeanne Marie Guyon, who was imprisoned in the Bastille because of her religious beliefs.

*   *   *

WHEN GOD GOES TO JAIL

JOSEPH was in prison. He was there not because he had done wrong but because he had done right. Because he had repulsed the advances of the wife of Potiphar, his master, she had lied about him and had falsely accused him; and he had, therefore, been thrown into prison.

The thirty-ninth chapter of Genesis, which tells the story, says, "And he was there in the prison. But the Lord was with Joseph." It is better to be in jail and have God with you than it is to be out of jail and without God. It is better to have a body in prison and the soul free than it is to have a body free and the soul in the prison of sin. "The steps of a good man are ordered by the Lord" (Psalm 37:23), and if, as a good man, your steps are ordered of God to jail, God will share your prison cell. The presence of God can transform a dungeon into a colony of heaven, but a palace without His presence and without His love to bless it may be a bit of hell itself.

This is not the day—at least in America—when it is common for men to be put into prison for refusing to do evil. There are, however, other surroundings in life just as unpleasant as a cell, and there are circumstances in life just as confining as the bolts and bars of a prison. The God whose presence made Joseph's time of imprisonment a time of blessing for him and a time of ministry to others, will, if our lives are yielded to Him, bless us and make us a source of blessing wherever we may be.

From his prison Joseph went to a position of power in Egypt second only to the king's. The God who was with him in prison went with him to the palace. In the day of his prominence and wealth Joseph remained faithful to God as he had been while in jail. I wonder if that was not the real test of the quality of his faith and spiritual experience. Many a man who enjoys the blessings of fellowship with the Most High in the time of disappointment and sorrow and poverty forgets Him amid wealth and prosperity and prominence.

> How tedious and tasteless the hours
>   When Jesus no longer I see;
> Sweet prospects, sweet birds, and sweet flowers
>   Have all lost their sweetness to me;
> The midsummer sun shines but dim,
>   The fields strive in vain to look gay;
> But when I am happy in Him,
>   December's as pleasant as May.
>
> His Name yields the richest perfume,
>   And sweeter than music His voice;
> His presence disperses my gloom,
>   And makes all within me rejoice;
> I should, were He always thus nigh,
>   Have nothing to wish or to fear;
> No mortal so happy as I,
>   My summer would last all the year.
>
> Content with beholding His face,
>   My all to His pleasure resigned,
> No changes of season or place
>   Would make any change in my mind:

While blest with a sense of His love,
A palace a toy would appear;
And prisons would palaces prove,
If Jesus would dwell with me there.

—*John Newton*

* * *

HABITS

WHAT you are is revealed not so much by what you do on special occasions as by what you do habitually. Habits develop through constant repetition of an act. Behind an act is a thought. Character is built act upon act and thought upon thought as a building rises stone upon stone. Habits reveal character because they indicate the process of the thinking. That which has become such a part of you that you do it unconsciously and habitually reveals what you are. Psychology has discovered this truth, but it was truth before modern "wise men" stumbled upon it. It is the truth set forth over and over in the Word of God: "As he thinketh in his heart, so is he" (Proverbs 23:7); "Keep thy heart with all diligence; for out of it are the issues of life" (Proverbs 4:23); "A good man out of the good treasure of the heart bringeth forth good things: and an evil man out of the evil treasure bringeth forth evil things" (Matthew 12:35).

Abraham lived habitually in such close communion with God that it became the most natural thing in the world for Abraham to set up an altar for sacrifice wherever he pitched his tent. David forgave his enemies so often that it became a natural part of his character to be forgiving. Moses was habitually so patient that we scarcely notice all the manifestations of patience in the life of this man whom the Bible describes as "very meek, above all the men which were upon the face of the earth" (Numbers 12:3). We notice his act of anger in smiting the rock (Numbers 20:11) for the very reason that it is so unlike him. The obedience to God's command which is natural for the old Prophet Samuel had its roots in the obedience of the young lad Samuel.

Something of the nature of our Lord Himself may be seen in the casual phrase, "as his custom was, he went into the synagogue" (Luke 4:16).

Habits are important whether they be habits of action or the habits of thought which precede the action, but the grace and power of God are sufficient to break the strong chain of evil habit and of wicked thinking. He is able to create a clean heart and renew a right spirit within. He can destroy the power of sinful habits. Indeed, He is able to regenerate completely, to make over the entire life.

> Searcher of Hearts!—from mine erase
> All thoughts that should not be,
> And in its deep recesses trace
> My gratitude to Thee!
>
> Hearer of Prayer!—oh, guide aright
> Each word and deed of mine;
> Life's battle teach me how to fight,
> And be the victory Thine.
>
> Giver of All! — for every good
> In the Redeemer came—
> For raiment, shelter and for food,
> I thank Thee in His Name.
>
> Father and Son and Holy Ghost!
> Thou glorious Three in One!
> Thou knowest best what I need most,
> And let Thy will be done.
>
> —*George Pope Morris*

*　　*　　*

GOD'S CURE FOR FAINTING SPELLS

LUKE tells us that the Lord spoke one of His parables to convey to His hearers the truth "that men ought always to pray, and not to faint" (Luke 18:1).

We think of prayer as a privilege, which certainly it is. One of the great miracles of God's grace is the fact that man may enjoy in prayer communion with God, that in prayer man may make his desires known to God, that he may in prayer discover God's will and ask God's intervention in his affairs.

But prayer is more than a privilege. It is an obligation. Each individual in the universe has a responsibility to do his best. Every father has a responsibility to be the best possible father to his child. Every child has a responsibility to his parents which it is his duty to meet to the best of his ability. Every businessman has an obligation of honor and integrity and industry, and it is the plain teaching of the Word of God that it is a sin for a man to do less than his best. No one can do his best until he taps the resources of Deity and seeks divine guidance. Prayer is, therefore, an obligation. Christians are commanded to "pray without ceasing," that is, to maintain a constant attitude of prayer, to keep in constant communion and fellowship with the Father. Paul more than once urged the saints to pray for him; and to Timothy, his son in the Gospel, he declared, "I will therefore that men pray everywhere, lifting up holy hands, without wrath and doubting" (I Timothy 2:8).

Prayer is instinctive. Men who have professed to doubt the existence of Deity in the midst of great battle or in a storm at sea have cried out to God when death seemed imminent. How much better to be in constant communion and fellowship with Him, regenerated children of God, making our desires and requests known unto Him, who is our Father, assured that "like as a father pitieth his children, so the Lord pitieth them that fear him" (Psalm 103:13).

> Lord, what a change within us one short hour
> Spent in Thy presence will avail to make!
> What heavy burdens from our bosoms take!
> What parchèd ground refresh as with a shower!
> We kneel, and all around us seems to lower;

We rise, and all, the distant and the near,
Stands forth in sunny outline, brave and clear;
We kneel, how weak! we rise, how full of power!
Why, therefore, should we do ourselves this wrong,
Or other—that we are not always strong—
That we are sometimes overborne with care—
That we should ever weak or heartless be,
Anxious or troubled—when with us is prayer,
And joy and strength and courage are with Thee?
—*Richard C. Trench*

* * *

THE STATE OF CONTENTMENT

THE "State of Contentment" is thinly populated. Few people know when they are well off. Most of us are like the children of Israel during their years in the wilderness.

They had been freed from slavery in Egypt. Their backs were scarred by the lashes which the taskmasters had laid upon them there. Their hands were still calloused with the toil of their slavery. Here in the wilderness they were free men out of whom God was building a nation. His tabernacle had been established in their midst. His presence had been shown by the pillar of fire by night and cloud by day. His law had been given them by His hand. Their clothes and their shoes were being miraculously preserved from wear. They were being fed by manna from heaven. It was no longer necessary for them to labor for the Egyptian taskmaster and feed upon the meal of slaves wearily prepared after the hard labor of the day. They had simply to pick up the manna God generously poured out each day.

But they grew tired of manna and began to long for the fleshpots of Egypt. They complained about God's menu and for the sake of the pleasure of their palates wished themselves back under the bondage of Pharaoh. They had forgotten the sting of the lash and the cruelty of the Egyptians. All they remembered was the odor of cooking meat.

It would seem that their hearts would have been so full of thanksgiving and praise that there would have been no room for complaint. But these Israelites are not the only ones who have lacked the virtue of contentment. Some even of the godly have need to pray for a contented heart, without which no man ever truly possesses all that God intends him to have of blessing. "Godliness with contentment is great gain" (I Timothy 6:6).

A little bird I am,
  Shut in from fields of air,
And in my cage I sit and sing
  To Him who placed me there;
Well pleased a prisoner to be,
Because, my God, it pleases Thee!

Naught have I else to do;
  I sing the whole day long;
And He whom I most love to please
  Doth listen to my song;
He caught and bound my wandering wing,
And still He bends to hear me sing.

Thou hast an ear to hear.
  A heart to love and bless;
And though my notes were e'er so rude,
  Thou wouldst not hear the less;
Because Thou knowest as they fall,
That love, sweet love, inspires them all.

My cage confines me round,
  Abroad I cannot fly;
But though my wing is closely bound,
  My heart's at liberty;
My prison walls cannot control
The flight, the freedom of the soul.

Oh, it is good to soar,
  These bolts and bars above,
To Him whose purpose I adore,
  Whose providence I love;
And in Thy mighty will to find
The joy, the freedom of the mind.
  —*Madame Guyon* (*written in the Bastille*)

"THE THING WE FORGET WITH"

SOMEONE asked a little boy what his memory was. He replied, "My memory is the thing I forget with." His definition accurately describes the memories of some of us with regard to the blessings and benefits of almighty God. Benisons are poured out upon us. We quickly forget.

As one reads the history of Israel in the Old Testament he finds abundant evidence of man's tendency to forget God's goodness. God brought Israel out of Egypt; He overthrew the power of Pharaoh, the mighty monarch, the ruler of a great nation; he sent plagues upon the land in order to set the people free. Pharaoh and his army were destroyed in the Red Sea. Surely, these happenings were sufficient evidence that the God who brought them out of Egypt was a God who was abundantly able to protect His chosen people and give them the land which He had appointed for them, but when they sent spies into the land, they came back with stories of walled cities, "fenced up to heaven," of giants in the land — powerful, mighty men. All the spies except Caleb and Joshua advised Israel not to attempt to capture the land. They forgot the power of God, so impressed were they with the physique of the giants. The people accepted their advice and the fear which the spies felt became the fear of the whole nation. For forty years Israel wandered in the wilderness until the entire generation died because they forgot the mercy and power of God manifested in their delivery from Egypt.

No wonder, then, that in the book of Deuteronomy the Lord urged Israel to "well remember what the Lord thy God did unto Pharaoh, and unto all Egypt" (Deuteronomy 7:18). The very laws which God instituted, the very ceremonies which He established for the government of His people and for their worship of Him, were to remind them of His power and His grace and His love. God said to them, "When thy son asketh thee in time to come, saying,

What mean the testimonies, and the statutes, and the judgments, which the Lord our God hath commanded you? Then thou shalt say unto thy son, We were Pharaoh's bondmen in Egypt; and the Lord brought us out of Egypt with a mighty hand" (Deuteronomy 6:20, 21).

God is faithful and never forgets His own. How His heart must be grieved at our forgetting Him! Over and over again He has proved that His grace is sufficient to meet all our needs, yet new trials bring new fears unassuaged by the memory of past blessing. How much happier we would be, how strong to meet the responsibilities of each day, if we would take as our motto and put into practice those words in the fourth verse of the first chapter of the Song of Solomon, "We will remember thy love."

> Though I forget Him and wander away,
> Yet doth He love me wherever I stray,
> Back to His dear loving arms would I flee,
> When I remember that Jesus loves me.

* * *

"Rejoice in the Lord Alway"
Philippians 4:4

FULLNESS OF JOY

To THE unsaved man or woman the Christian way of life seems gloomy and unhappy. In their opinion, when one becomes a Christian he gives up things which are pleasant and attractive and undertakes a life of long-faced monotony and pious misery. Nothing could be further from the truth. The Christian life is a way of happiness. Faith in Christ implants joy in the human heart. The Saviour came that men might have abundant life, and a life without joy is certainly not abundant; it is barren and empty. The Apostle Peter speaks of the Lord as the One in whom "believing, ye rejoice with joy unspeakable and full of glory" (I Peter 1:8). The heart of a child of God has every reason to rejoice. The Christian rejoices because of what Christ has given him and because of what He has taken away. He has been given salvation. He has passed from death into life. He has been given the assurance of God's presence now and hereafter. From him has been removed a sense of guilt and a weight of sin. He has been freed from the domination of old habits and old impulses. He has been led out of darkness into light. Surely, this is enough to cause springs of joy to well up in the heart.

A day-by-day experience of God's mercy develops the Christian's joy. As he trusts his Lord for comfort in the time of sorrow and finds the comfort supplied, as he leans upon Him for strength in a moment of weakness and finds himself upheld, as he turns to Him in the hour of need and finds the need met, he cannot help rejoicing.

This joy is increased as the Lord speaks to him through His Word, the Bible. Christ Himself said to His disciples, "These things have I spoken unto you, that my joy might remain in you, and that your joy might be full" (John 15:11), and from the Word of God a joy ever new and fresh comes to the Christian as he turns the holy pages. The command to rejoice seems almost superfluous as he is told to "rejoice in the Lord alway" (Philippians 4:4). When he walks with His Father, the Christian is always filled with joy.

> Jesus, Thou joy of loving hearts,
> Thou fount of life, Thou light of men,
> From all the bliss that earth imparts
> We turn unfilled to Thee again.
>
> Thy truth unchanged hath ever stood;
> Thou savest those that on Thee call;
> To them that seek Thee Thou art good,
> To them that find Thee, all in all.
>
> Our restless spirits yearn for Thee,
> Where'er our changeful lot is cast;
> Glad, when Thy gracious smile we see,
> Blest, when our faith can hold Thee fast.
>
> O Jesus, ever with us stay;
> Make all our moments calm and bright;
> Chase the dark night of sin away,
> Shed o'er the world Thy holy light!
>
> —*Bernard of Clairvaux*

* * *

HIS OWN GOD

David was a man after God's own heart, but he was not free from sorrow and suffering. His life was often in danger and he knew what it meant to be pursued by an enemy and lose temporal possessions. One of the occasions when, from the human standpoint, he should have been in the lowest emotional state is recorded in the thirtieth chapter of I Samuel. David had returned with his soldiers to his city of Ziklag to find it in ruins. The Amalekites had carried away their wives and their children and their possessions. His discouraged followers broke into open rebellion. There is no record that David was discouraged in this hour. On the contrary, we are told, "David encouraged himself in the Lord his God" (I Samuel 30:6). God was real and personal to David. God was *his* God. Only the man who has established a personal relationship with God is prepared to meet the loss of loved ones and possessions as David met it. Only the man who has made God his own can encourage himself in God in such an hour.

The God whom David knew as his God was the God of Abraham, Isaac, and Jacob. He was the God of Israel, but most important of all to David, He was *his* God. It is well to recognize the existence of God in His universe, but we need to know Him *personally*. We need to make Him *our* God. He wants us each to come into personal relationship with Him. "But if from thence thou shalt seek the Lord thy God, thou shalt find him, if thou seek him with all thy heart and with all thy soul" (Deuteronomy 4:29). The Lord Jesus Christ, who is God come in the flesh and the Way by which men may come to God, said, "Behold, I stand at the door, and knock: if any man hear my voice, and open the door, I will come in to him, and will sup with him, and he with me" (Revelation 3:20).

The Amalekites took all David's earthly possessions, but they could not take God away from him. In the midst of his loss he kept that which was most important—a personal grip on God. In the midst of causes for discouragement he had kept his source of encouragement—his God.

> I love, my God, but with no love of mine,
> For I have none to give;
> I love Thee, Lord, but all that love is Thine,
> For by Thy life I live.
> I am as nothing, and rejoice to be
> Emptied and lost and swallowed up in Thee.

Thou, Lord, alone, art all Thy children need
  And there is none beside;
From Thee the streams of blessedness proceed;
  In Thee the blest abide,
Fountain of life and all-abounding grace,
Our source, our center and our dwelling-place!
                                —*Madame Guyon*

*   *   *

FAITH OR CONFIDENCE

SOME people confuse faith with confidence. In one sense, the two are not identical in their source, nor are they founded on a common spiritual basis.

Confidence may be born of a nature that is naturally optimistic and hopes for the best. A man may be confident that "things will turn out all right," and think he has faith when he has only confidence.

Confidence may spring from a knowledge of the characteristics and potentialities which another possesses. A mother may have confidence in the qualities of her son's character and take it for granted that because of them he will make a success of his life, and think she has faith.

Confidence may spring from reliance upon oneself. A man may evaluate his own gifts and talents and abilities and have confidence that he will be able to accomplish a certain task and think this is faith.

Faith is more than this. Faith is fixed in God. Faith is not merely an unreasoning hope, nor is it wishful thinking that God will do the thing we want Him to do. It is the assurance that He will keep His word and bring to pass that which He has promised to perform. Faith is founded in God who *can* because He is omnipotent, and who *will* because He promised. The surrendered Christian knows that God will lead him because he believes the Word of God which promises, "Commit thy way unto the Lord; trust also in him; and he shall bring it to pass" Psalm 37:5). A godly mother has faith that her child will live right because she has done her best to bring him up in the fear of the Lord and because God has assured her in His Word, "Train up a child in the way he should go: and when he is old, he will not depart from it" (Proverbs 22:6).

Faith is superior to confidence as divine omnipotence is superior to mortal weakness. Confidence may enable a man to climb a mountain whose lofty peak challenges his efforts. Faith removes the mountain. Confidence helps a mariner to sail his boat safely through a stormy sea, but only faith can enable a man to walk on the waves. Faith has this foundation — the Word of God — and "the foundation [Word] of God standeth sure."

> Faith is a living power from heaven
> That grasps the promise God hath given,
> A trust that cannot be o'erthrown,
> Fixed heartily on Christ alone.
>
> Faith finds in Christ whate'er we need
> To save or strengthen us indeed;
> Receive the grace He sends us down,
> And makes us share His cross and crown.
>
> Faith in the conscience worketh peace
> And bids the mourner's weeping cease;
> By faith the children's place we claim,
> And give all honor to one Name.
>
> Faith feels the Spirit's kindling breath
> In love and hope that conquer death;
> Faith worketh hourly joy in God,
> And trusts and blesses e'en the rod.
>
> We thank Thee, then, O God of heaven,
> That Thou to us this faith hast given
> In Jesus Christ Thy Son, who is
> Our only fount and source of bliss.
> —*Petrus Herbert*

BE NOT AFRAID

ON TWO OCCASIONS (Mark 4:35-39; Matthew 14:22-27)
the Lord's disciples were caught in a storm on the Sea of
Galilee. The first time Jesus was asleep in the stern of
the boat. In their fear they waked Him, asking, "Carest
thou not that we perish?" He arose and rebuked the wind
and said to the waves, "Be still." With the simple language
of divine authority He silenced the tempest and calmed the
sea. The waves, like little dogs that obey the command
of their master, lay down and went to sleep.

On the other occasion the disciples were in the boat without Him, and in the midst of the tempest He came to them
walking on the sea. This time He did not speak to the wind
or the sea, but to them. "It is I; be not afraid." He had
demonstrated His power over the storm once. Now His
very presence should bring them confidence.

Christ is still able to quiet the tempest and subdue storms.
He can still work the miracle of bringing peace and quiet
out of turmoil and discord, but it is not always His will
to do so. When He permits the storm to rage, His very
presence in the lives of those who know and love Him brings
peace and confidence in the midst of the storm. It is a
wonderful thing to know the Saviour, who is able to settle
strife and subdue discord and bring peace out of tumult. It
is even more wonderful to have a Lord who can give inward
peace and confidence to His followers in the midst of the
storm it is not His divine will to subdue. Into every life
comes a time of tempest when the winds blow and the
waves beat and the seas threaten to engulf. In such a time
the very presence of the Saviour is able to impart within
our souls a sense of security and calm in amazing contrast
to the tempest about us. In the midst of the storm which
He permits to rage, He comes to His own, walking on the
very waves which would become still if He should so command. He does not address the raging elements. He speaks

instead to the frightened and storm-tossed ones. Above the sound of the storm and the surge of the seas comes the melody of His voice, "It is I; be not afraid," and all is quiet and peaceful within their breasts. So amid the storms of our lives He speaks to His own, "My peace I give unto you: not as the world giveth, give I unto you. Let not your heart be troubled, neither let it be afraid" (John 14:27).

> No coward soul is mine,
> No trembler in the world's storm-troubled sphere:
> I see heaven's glories shine,
> And faith shines equal, arming me from fear.
>
> O God within my breast,
> Almighty, ever-present Deity!
> Life — that in me hast rest,
> As I—undying Life—have power in Thee!
> —*Emily Brontë*

* * *

AS A STRING AROUND GOD'S FINGER

WHEN the flood was over, the waters had receded, and the Ark had settled on the dry ground, God made a covenant with Noah and his sons that never would "all flesh be cut off any more by the waters of a flood." The word *covenant* is one of the wonderful words of the Bible and it means literally "a coming together." It signifies a voluntary promise, a pledge made by God to His creatures. The very word speaks of divine mercy and grace and condescension.

God not only made a promise to Noah, but He also sets the sign of His covenant in the heavens for men of every generation to behold. Indeed, this covenant has been called the *Rainbow Covenant,* for God promised Noah that when the storm clouds gather His bow shall be set in the clouds and God said, "I will look upon it, that I may remember the everlasting covenant between God and every living creature" (Genesis 9:16). God pins the ribbon of the rainbow upon the breast of the storm cloud to remind Him of His covenant to man. Whenever God looks upon the rainbow it reminds Him of the promise that He made, though man may see the rainbow only as an arch of color across the sky, a thing of beauty, forgetting that it is a sign of God's faithfulness.

Men forget God so easily. They accept the blessings which He gives with never a thought of the Giver. They live for themselves with no regard for the Author of life. Or, in times of trouble and distress and special conviction, they make promises to the Lord which they forget with the passing of the days. Men are faithless and forgetful, but God remembers and keeps His covenant. God's promises are fixed and sure. However faithless we may prove, He is still the Faithful One.

The promises of God's judgment are as sure as the covenant of His mercy. Just as surely as He will save and redeem —as He has promised to—those who trust Him, so surely will He keep His word by punishing those who mock sin and reject the atoning blood of His Son.

> When all Thy mercies, O my God,
>   My rising soul surveys,
> Transported with the view, I'm lost
>   In wonder, love and praise.
>
> Unnumbered comforts to my soul
>   Thy tender care bestowed,
> Before my infant heart conceived
>   From whom those comforts flowed.
>
> When worn with sickness, oft hast Thou
>   With health renewed my face,
> And, when in sins and sorrows sunk,
>   Revived my soul with grace.
>
> Ten thousand, thousand precious gifts
>   My daily thanks employ,
> Nor is the least a cheerful heart
>   That tastes those gifts with joy.
>   —*Joseph Addison*

"TIGHTWADS"

THERE are many people to whom the Bible refers whose names do not appear in the record. Often the casual reader fails to notice these minor actors in the great dramas of the Bible. Such are those individuals mentioned in connection with the procuring of the donkey upon which Christ rode into Jerusalem a few days before His crucifixion.

He sent the disciples into the village with the instructions that they would find "an ass tied, and a colt with her" (Matthew 21:2). They were to be loosed and brought to Him. Should any inquire what they were doing, the disciples were to answer, "The Lord hath need of them" (Matthew 21:3). The disciples went and found the animals at a corner where two roads met. As they took them, some who stood by asked, "What do ye, loosing the colt?" (Mark 11:5), and when the disciples replied as the Lord had instructed, they let them go.

Who these bystanders may have been we do not know. Possibly the owner of the animals was one of them or they may have been members of his family or his servants or friends. They must have been acquainted with the disciples whom they had surely seen before with Christ. Evidently they at least knew who the disciples were. Certainly they were good men, for all they needed was to be told that the Lord needed the animals and they let them go willingly.

They are different from some folk I know, who refuse God the use of the very things which He has given to them. There are those who hold on to their money and refuse to support the work of the Lord. They deny God their time and their talents though every breath of their lives He supplies, and the power to make money, He endowed them with, and their talents He entrusted to them.

We do not know the name of the owner of the beast upon which Christ rode into Jerusalem, but we all know the names of some who under the same circumstances would have said, "But the animals belong to me. They are too valuable to give the Lord."

> What was his name? I do not know his name;
> I only know he heard God's voice and came,
>   Brought all he had across the sea
>   To live and work for God and me;
>   Felled the ungracious oak;
>   Dragged from the soil
>   With horrid toil
>   The thrice-gnarled roots and stubborn rock;
> With plenty piled the haggard mountain side;
> And at the end, without memorial, died.
> No blaring trumpets sounded out his fame,
> He lived—he died—I do not know his name.
>
> And I?
> Is there some desert or some pathless sea
> Where Thou, Good God of angels, wilt send me?
>   Some oak for me to rend; some sod,
>   Some rock for me to break;
>   Some handful of His corn to take
>   And scatter far afield,
>   Till it, in turn, shall yield
>   Its hundredfold
>   Of grains of gold
>   To feed the waiting children of my God?
> Show me the desert, Father, or the sea.
> Is it Thine enterprise? Great God, send me.
> And though this body lie where ocean rolls,
> Count me among all faithful souls.
>   —*Edward Everett Hale*

*　　*　　*

"MY JOY . . . IN YOU"

ON THE night of the Last Supper, Jesus, as He spoke to His disciples about His relationship with the Father and their relationship with Him and as He discussed with them their attitude toward the world, said, "These things have I spoken unto you, that my joy might remain in you, and that your joy might be full" (John 15:11).

When the joy of the Lord Jesus Christ is in a man's heart his joy is always full, and there is no fullness of joy anywhere except in Christ. God has made the human heart so only He Himself can fill it. All the pleasures of the world, all the riches of earth, though they may bring a temporary thrill, leave unsatisfied the longing of the heart. "My heart and my flesh crieth out for the living God," says the psalmist. The soul of man is immortal, and only God can satisfy the hunger of the soul and bring eternal joy. The immortal cannot be satisfied with the temporal, and the eternal with that which is transient. Some of the most unhappy people I have known have been people of wealth and fame—people successful from the viewpoint of the world. Some of the happiest people I know are those who have little of the material things of life, no fame and no prominence, but who possess the unsearchable riches of Christ. Of course, the Christian has his sorrows. He is grieved by the deaths of his loved ones, but he sorrows not "as those who have no hope," and in the midnight of his sorrow sings the nightingale of hope bringing joy to his heart with the assurance that he shall see his dear ones again.

When the man without Christ loses his wealth and his friends and his family, he has lost everything. Let the Christian see his family taken from him, his temporal possessions swept away and his friends removed—he still has the abiding presence of Christ in whom his hope is fixed and who is the Author and Source of his joy. The man whose affections are set on Christ has every reason to rejoice because he knows that all things work together for his good (Romans 8:28). The man who lives in daily fellowship with the Lord is in contact with the Source of joy eternal. "In thy presence is fulness of joy; at thy right hand there are pleasures for evermore" (Psalm 16:11).

Think—
Of stepping on shore, and finding it heaven!
Of taking hold of a hand, and finding it God's hand.
Of breathing a new air, and finding it celestial air.
Of feeling invigorated, and finding it immortality.
Of passing from storm and tempest to an unbroken calm.
Of waking up, and finding it Home.

—Anonymous

*   *   *

LIGHT FOR OUR DARKNESS

NONE of the statements which the Lord Jesus made of Himself is more emphatic than this, "I am the light of the world." No assurance which He gives to man is more positive than this, "he that followeth me shall not walk in darkness."

He is Light and the Author of light. By Him were all things made. His hands lighted starry tapers, and at His word were born the blazing suns of the universe. In Him there is no darkness at all—no darkness of ignorance, for He knows the end from the beginning; no darkness of death, for He is the Light of Life; no darkness of sin, for He is the Sun of Righteousness; no darkness of error, for He is Truth Incarnate. Heaven itself finds in Him the source of its light. John on the isle of Patmos catching a glimpse of the beauty and effulgent glory of the New Jerusalem, wrote, "And the city had no need of the sun, neither of the moon, to shine in it: for the glory of God did lighten it, and the Lamb is the light thereof. And the nations of them which are saved shall walk in the light of it" (Revelation 21:23, 24).

The man who follows Christ never walks in darkness. He may walk in the midst of darkness, but his steps are lighted by the presence of the Saviour whom he follows, just as a man who walks on a dark night behind a guide with a lantern finds, in the midst of the darkness, light in the spot where he walks. The man who follows Christ has the light of divine wisdom cast upon the problems which confront him, and in this light he is able to solve them. He may not be able to see the future or view the long way stretching ahead, but there is light where he needs it, when he needs it, in the very spot where he finds himself. In the night of great sorrow the man who follows Christ finds the light of hope to cheer his way. Christ proves Himself the true light to all who follow Him.

> Christ, whose glory fills the skies,
>   Christ the true, the only light,
> Sun of Righteousness, arise,
>   Triumph o'er the shades of night;
> Dayspring from on high, be near;
> Daystar, in my heart appear.
> Dark and cheerless is the morn
>   Unaccompanied by Thee;
> Joyless is the day's return,
>   Till Thy mercy's beams I see,
> Till thy inward light impart,
> Glad my eyes and warm my heart.
> Visit, then, this soul of mine,
>   Pierce the gloom of sin and grief;
> Fill me, Radiancy divine,
>   Scatter all my unbelief;
> More and more Thyself display,
> Shining to the perfect day.
> —*Charles Wesley*

*   *   *

TIME MARCHES ON

THE armies of Israel were in the midst of a battle with the Ammonites. Victory seemed to be at hand, but there were not enough hours of daylight left in which to follow up the advantage they were gaining and destroy the Ammonite armies. Joshua, the leader chosen by God for Israel, confident in the strength of His Lord and assured that it was God's will for Israel to wipe out her enemies, commanded the sun to stand still. In obedience to his command the progress of the sun toward the west was stayed. The day was lengthened and Israel was victorious.

How many times we have wished for Joshua's power over the forces of nature! How often we have longed to lengthen the hours that have been full of joy and pleasure! Who has not wished for more time to complete his tasks and accomplish the purposes he has had to cram into hours all too short?

Who has not, at other times, wished that he could reverse the process and speed the fleeting hours? Time hangs heavily about a bed of pain. The minutes march with lagging steps through the dark valley of sorrow. For the lover the days limp like laggards along the lonely path of separation from the one he loves.

Who has not wished that he could reverse the journeyings of the sun and bring back again the days of childhood and hours long since lost in the sea of eternity? Who has not cried in his soul, "Backward, turn backward, O Time, in thy flight"?

We are not Joshuas. To us is not given to lengthen the day or to shorten it. We cannot recall lost hours, but we can fill each day. We can pack into each hour and each moment faithful service and profitable accomplishment. We cannot lengthen the hours, but we must not waste the minutes. "Art is long and time is fleeting," and some time we must give an account to God for the investment we have made of the days and the hours and the moments entrusted to us.

> "Why sit'st thou by that ruined hall,
>   Thou aged carle so stern and gray?
> Dost thou its former pride recall,
>   Or ponder how it passed away?"

"Know'st thou not me?" the Deep Voice cried:
  "So long enjoyed, so oft misused—
Alternate, in thy fickle pride,
  Desired, neglected, and accused!

Before my breath, like blazing flax,
  Man and his marvels pass away!
And changing empires wane and wax,
  Are founded, flourish and decay.

Redeem mine hours—the space is brief—
  While in my glass the sand-grains shiver,
And measureless thy joy or grief,
  When Time and thou shalt part forever!"
                              —*The Antiquary*

*   *   *

OUR ARMAMENTS AND HIS ARM

WISE words these from the book of Proverbs, "The horse is prepared against the day of battle: but safety is of the Lord" (Proverbs 21:31). We have had abundant evidence of the folly of being unprepared for the attack of the aggressor. The Great War brought upon the freedom-loving nations of the world defeat after defeat because they were not prepared. Trained soldiers were lacking. Equipment was lacking. Armaments were lacking.

It is a wise thing for a nation to be prepared for war when it comes, but armies and arms do not themselves assure victory. "The race is not to the swift, nor the battle to the strong" (Ecclesiastes 9:11). The God of battles oftentimes fights on the side which is weaker in numbers and equipment. The walls of Jericho did not go down under the bombardment of heavy artillery but before the blasts of priestly trumpets and the shouts of faith. Israel was not freed from the menace of the Egyptian by a blitzkrieg of mechanized troops but by the waters of the Red Sea, which

God poured in upon Pharaoh's army. Goliath was not destroyed by a veteran equipped with all the paraphernalia of war but by a shepherd lad with faith in his heart and a sling in his hand. Three hundred men under Gideon, the Lord's captain, were victorious over an army of 135,000.

It is wise to be prepared, but it is foolish to trust only in arms and fail to take into account the power of God in whose strong arm victory resides. "If God be for us, who can be against us?" (Romans 8:31). Our faith, our trust, our hope should be in the "Lord strong and mighty, the Lord mighty in battle." We should be as wise as David who said, "Some trust in chariots, and some in horses: but we will remember the name of the Lord our God" (Psalm 20:7). God has yet to fail those whose faith and trust is fixed in Him. It is our responsibility to do everything in our power to defeat the enemy and achieve victory. It is our privilege to trust in Him who is of nations as of men: Rock, Fortress, Deliverer, Strength, Buckler, Horn of Salvation and High Tower (Psalm 18:2).

> I greet Thee, my Redeemer sure,
>   I trust in none but Thee,
> Thou who hast borne such toil and shame
>   And suffering for me:
> Our hearts from cares and cravings vain
>   And foolish fears set free.
>
> Thou art the King compassionate,
>   Thou reignest everywhere;
> Almighty Lord, reign Thou in us,
>   Rule all we have and are:
> Enlighten us and raise to heaven,
>   Amid Thy glories there.
>
> Thou art the life by which we live;
>   Our stay and strength's in Thee;
> Uphold us so in face of death,
>   What time soe'er it be,
> That we may meet it with strong heart,
>   And may die peacefully.

Look Thou, our Daysman and High Priest,
　Upon our low estate;
Make us to see God's face in peace
　Through Thee, our Advocate;
With Thee, our Saviour, may our feet
　Enter at heaven's gate.

—John Calvin

* * *

PRAYER THAT GETS THROUGH

THE best prayer is not always the best-worded prayer. A man can build a rhetorical structure of phrase upon phrase ornamented with all the embellishments of language, address it to Deity, intone it solemnly and call it a prayer, and it may never go higher than the ceiling.

Real prayer gushes from the heart. It is the spontaneous outflowing of deep desire in petition to God. A child who greatly desires something asks his father for it without thinking particularly of the language he uses. He says simply, "Daddy, I want that. Give it to me." Waking frightened in the darkness, a child does not consider the tone of voice that he uses when he calls to his mother. Similarly, true prayer pours from the heart of our need and the depths of our desire to God.

An interesting verse in the Old Testament tells us that the men of Judah in the midst of a battle found themselves surrounded by their enemies and "they cried unto the Lord" (II Chronicles 13:14). There was no time to compose formal prayers. The soldiers of Judah needed help and needed it quickly, and they cried unto God. It may be doubted whether they were conscious of the words that they used. They may not have formed words at all, but the chapter tells us that God heard them and smote their enemies and delivered them into the hands of those busy, fighting Judeans, who cried out to Him in the midst of the battle.

The man in the heat of a battle praying for deliverance does not choose his words carefully. The man who is oppressed by a consciousness of his sin and need is not concerned with how he sounds when he cries, "God be merciful to me a sinner."

> From ev'ry stormy wind that blows,
> From ev'ry swelling tide of woes,
> There is a calm, a sure retreat;
> 'Tis found beneath the mercy-seat.
>
> There is a place where Jesus sheds
> The oil of gladness on our heads,
> A place than all beside more sweet;
> It is the blood-bo't mercy-seat.
>
> There is a scene where spirits blend,
> Where friend holds fellowship with friend;
> Tho' sundered far, by faith they meet
> Around one common mercy-seat.
>
> There, there on eagle's wings we soar,
> And sin and sense seem all no more,
> And heav'n comes down our souls to greet,
> And glory crowns the mercy-seat.
>
> —*Hugh Stowell*

*   *   *

"YE ASK AND RECEIVE NOT"

GOD, who is a God of law and order, has set certain conditions upon the fulfillment of which depends His promise to hear and answer our prayers.

First, we must have pure hearts. "If I regard iniquity in my heart, the Lord will not hear me" (Psalm 66:18). This means that the man who continually practices sin and who has in his heart a purpose to commit sin, and who clings to sin, has no claim upon the ear of God.

Prayer that God promises to answer must come also from an unselfish heart. "Ye ask, and receive not, because ye ask amiss, that ye may consume it upon your lusts" (James 4:3). Man has no right to ask God for something which he wants to use merely for the gratification of his own desires or for his own personal satisfaction.

Prayer to be heard must come from a yielded heart— a heart submissive to God's will. "If we ask any thing according to his will he heareth us" (I John 5:14). A heart thus yielded will certainly be a heart that is pure and a heart that is unselfish. The life in which the will of God is foremost is a life which has no room for impurity and selfishness.

Prayer without faith God nowhere promises to answer. A believing heart is essential if we are to meet the conditions which God places upon our access to Him with our petitions. Jesus said to His disciples, "All things, whatsoever ye shall ask in prayer, believing, ye shall receive" (Matthew 21:22).

The Lord Jesus Christ said our prayers should be in His Name. "Whatsoever ye shall ask in my name, that will I do, that the Father may be glorified in the Son" (John 14:13). Only by faith in the Lord Jesus Christ are men saved. Only through His blood are sins washed away, and only in Him do we become children of God. How proper, therefore, that our prayers to our Father should be in the Name and for the sake of Him who has made our sonship possible. In Christ's Name we may bring our petitions to our Heavenly Father, and "he that spared not his own Son, but delivered him up for us all, how shall he not with him also freely give us all things?" (Romans 8:32).

> There is an eye that never sleeps
> Beneath the wing of night;
> There is an ear that never shuts
> When sink the beams of light.

There is an arm that never tires
 When human strength gives way;
There is a love that never fails
 When earthly loves decay.

That eye unseen o'erwatcheth all;
 That arm upholds the sky;
That ear doth hear the sparrow call;
 That love is ever nigh.

—James Cowden Wallace

* * *

"Be Not Afraid, But Speak"

Acts 18:9

FAITH AT WORK

THERE was a sick man who had some fine friends who did more than sympathize with him in his sickness and tell him that they felt sorry for him. They carried him to Jesus to be healed. When they came to the house in which the Lord was teaching, the crowd was so large that they could not get in, but, not to be discouraged, they climbed on the flat, Oriental roof, lifted several tiles and with ropes lowered the sick man on his bed until he lay at Jesus' feet.

The man was healed by the power of the Son of God, but his friends had a share in the healing. Except for their efforts he would never have been brought to the Saviour. Those men had evidently seen the miracles which He had performed on other sick bodies. They had faith that Christ could heal their friend. They gave evidence of that faith when they brought him to Christ; they gave evidence not only of faith but also of character and determination when they failed to let the crowd deter them in their efforts and defeat them in their purpose.

There are many Christian people who know the power of Christ today. They have felt the manifestation of His power in their own lives in the forgiveness of their sins. They have seen the demonstration of His power in the lives of others. They have friends who need the miraculous touch of Christ, who are living in sin, who are victims of habits which they cannot conquer and of evil which cripples them spiritually and morally; yet they never make an effort to bring these friends to Christ.

Every Christian has a responsibility to make Christ known to men, yet all too many Christians are so busy about business or pleasure or the pursuit of selfish ambition that they neglect to speak for the Lord or to bring those needy ones into His presence. Others set out to lead men to Christ but become discouraged before the task is done. Christians today need a determination that tears holes in roofs to bring poor, sin-sick men and women to the feet of the Saviour.

> Christian soul, the times are calling,
> Altars falling,
> Men's hearts failing them for fear;
> Unto thee their eyes are turning,
> Spirits yearning,
> For the word of faith and cheer.
>
> Christian soul, great deeds await thee,
> Consecrate thee
> To the task that nearest lies;
> Question not that God will use thee,
> Nor refuse thee
> Blessing on thy sacrifice.
>
> Walk thou not as one benighted,
> Nor affrighted,
> Where the foolish see no God;
> Thine to glimpse the fiery column,
> Thine the solemn
> Comfort of His staff and rod!
>
> —*Louise Betts Edwards*

* * *

NO UNION RULES

CHRIST said to Peter, "Feed my sheep" (John 21:16). That was a strange command to give Peter. Peter was not a shepherd. He was a fisherman. He was to follow Jesus and be a soul-winner, an evangelist. Christ's call to Peter had been to follow Him and be a fisher of men (Matthew 4:19), but the Saviour, just before ascending to heaven, gave to Peter this command to feed His sheep—the duty of the pastor, the shepherd.

The inference here is plain indeed. No disciple of the Lord is called to only one task and is completely free from the responsibility of every other. A child of God has the obligation of performing any service which he may find at hand.

The Bible plainly teaches that God has called every Christian to certain specific tasks and has given him the gifts and talents necessary for the successful performance of those tasks, but this does not relieve the Christian from obligations and duties outside his own particular field. Every Christian should be a soul-winner, though certainly all Christians are not called to be evangelists or pastors or foreign missionaries.

The Christian mother in her home has first of all a responsibility toward her own family and the duty of caring for her own children, but her obligations do not end here. Everywhere she goes she should by her life and actions testify for her Lord.

The Christian businessman has the responsibility of his business and the duty of providing for his family, but he has a responsibility beyond these. He is also obliged to witness and testify to the saving power of Christ. There is the duty of helping to finance the spread of the Gospel, and there is the obligation of the strong to bear the infirmities of the weak.

I have known Christians who were so interested in foreign missions that they neglected the opportunities at their front doors. I have known Christian men, occupied with the effort of earning a living and providing material comforts for their families, who allowed their own boys to grow up virtually as strangers to them, without the companionship which every son has a right to expect of his father.

Modern life is complex. No Christian in this day has only one responsibility. In using the particular gifts with which God has endowed us and in following the path of service to which we have been called, we sometimes forget that we have an obligation to take advantage of every opportunity for service and testimony which God sends our way in whatever field of endeavor it may be.

> Go, labor on! spend and be spent;
> Thy joy to do the Father's will:
> It is the way the Master went—
> Should not the servant tread it still?
>
> Go, labor on! 'tis not for nought,
> Thine earthly loss is heavenly gain;
> Men heed thee, love thee, praise thee not;
> The Master praises—what are men?
>
> Toil on, faint not, keep watch and pray;
> Be wise the erring soul to win;
> Go forth into the world's highway,
> Compel the wanderer to come in.
>
> Toil on, and in thy toil rejoice!
> For toil comes rest, for exile home;
> Soon shalt thou hear the Bridegroom's voice,
> The midnight peal, "Behold, I come!"
>
> —*Horatius Bonar*

* * *

IN STRANGE PLACES

THE Bible opens to the thoughtful reader rich treasure houses of thought with the golden key of a brief phrase. How the imagination is stimulated as one reads what Paul, writing to the Philippians from Rome, said: "All the saints salute you, chiefly they that are of Caesar's household" (Philippians 4:22).

What were they like—those Christians in Nero's palace? It seems strange to find saints members of Nero's official family. Were they poor slaves doing the menial tasks? Were they officers of his guard? Did they plan the meals and spread the banquets? Did one act as a scribe taking down the imperial decrees? Did another supervise the wardrobe of the empress? We may never know in this life anything specific about these unknown Christians from whom the apostle sent greetings. But this we do know, that even in the house of the inhuman monster Nero dwelt some of God's own children. In the midst of the corruption and licentiousness of Caesar's household were some of God's saints. Surrounded by the wickedness and depravity of as corrupt a court as ever rotted in its sin, there were some who served Christ and whose affections were fixed on heavenly things.

The Christian whose heart is firmly set to be true to God and whose eyes are fixed on Christ can stand true to his Lord no matter in what environment he has to live. God's children need not become defiled by the filth of the world nor corrupted with its deadly poison.

Meshach, Shadrach, Abednego and Daniel had been taken from their homeland to Babylon by Nebuchadnezzar. There in his palace they refused to defile themselves with the king's meat and drink of his wines. The first three were thrown into a fiery furnace rather than bow to the image set up by the king, and Daniel was cast into the den of lions rather than forsake even for a period of thirty days his time of prayer and communion with God.

The Christian who purposes in his heart to serve God has divine resources at his command. His God is a sovereign more powerful than any earthly king or emperor.

> Be Thou my Vision, O Lord of my heart;
> Naught be all else to me, save that Thou art—
> Thou my best thought, by day or by night,
> Waking or sleeping, Thy presence my light.
>
> Be Thou my Wisdom, and Thou my true Word;
> I ever with Thee and Thou with me, Lord;
> Thou my great Father, I Thy true son;
> Thou in me dwelling, and I with Thee one.
>
> Riches I heed not, nor man's empty praise,
> Thou mine inheritance, now and always;
> Thou and Thou only, first in my heart,
> High King of heaven, my treasure Thou art.

High King of heaven, my victory won,
May I reach heaven's joys, O bright heaven's Sun!
Heart of my own heart, whatever befall,
Still be my Vision, O Ruler of all.

—Ancient Irish Hymn

* * *

IDENTIFICATION TAG

PETER and John were arrested and brought before the Sanhedrin for preaching "through Jesus the resurrection from the dead" (Acts 4:2). These two fishermen were not frightened as they stood on trial before the very men who had condemned Jesus to death. Arrested for preaching to the people, they now preached to the Sanhedrin with such boldness and logic that when the council perceived that they were unlearned and "ignorant" men, "they marvelled; and they took knowledge of them, that they had been with Jesus" (Acts 4:13). These men, as His disciples, had followed God's Son for three years. They had lived in daily, close, personal contact with Him. Into the lives of these ordinary, lowly men had come a likeness to the Son of God.

One always becomes like his associates. A couple whose lives are blended together through years of marriage grow somewhat like each other. A student acquires not only something of the knowledge and the point of view of the teacher whom he admires, but ofttimes assumes something of his manner and peculiarities. The influence of our associates upon our lives it is impossible to measure, but that there is an influence no man can deny. In habits, in language, in thought itself we reflect those with whom we constantly mingle.

The man who walks with God becomes like God. The Christian who fellowships daily with the Saviour reveals to others in his own life a Christlike personality.

Paul, referring to the scars he had received as a result of persecution for Christ's sake, said, "I bear in my body the marks of the Lord Jesus" (Galatians 6:17). The Christian who is much with Christ will bear in his soul the marks of his Lord. Men, seeing the sweetness and power of his life, will take knowledge of him that he has been with Jesus.

> Our God is love; and all His saints
>   His image bear below:
> The heart with love to God inspired
>   With love to man will glow.
>
> Teach us to love each other, Lord,
>   As we are loved by Thee;
> None who are truly born of God
>   Can live in enmity.
>
> Heirs of the same immortal bliss,
>   Our hopes and fears the same,
> With bonds of love our hearts unite,
>   With mutual love inflame.
>
> So may the unbelieving world
>   See how true Christians love;
> And glorify our Saviour's grace,
>   And seek that grace to prove.
>   —*Thomas Cotterill*

* * *

BUILDING SILENTLY

THE world has seen few buildings as magnificent as Solomon's Temple, but one of the most amazing things about this structure was the complete silence which attended its building. "There was neither hammer nor axe nor any tool of iron heard in the house, while it was in building" (I Kings 6:7). The stones were dressed in the quarries. The cedar wood brought from Lebanon was prepared before its arrival on the Temple site. The metal work was brought already prepared and installed quietly.

Possibly back of this silence was a feeling of reverence.

This was God's house, a place for sacrifice to the Lord and for the worship of Jehovah. It was appropriate that it be built in an atmosphere of quiet reverence. Possibly efficiency and convenience were also reasons for building silently. With stones dressed and smoothed where they were quarried, it was unnecessary to transport surplus material which should be cut away and not used in the building.

The silence with which the huge and beautiful Temple was built is full of spiritual suggestion. It suggests the quiet way in which God works in carrying out His purposes in the world. The coming of the Lord Jesus Christ to reign will be a spectacular coming, but the preparation of His bride in the redemption of men and women throughout the world is quiet in comparison with the noise and tumult which attend less important movements.

The most important events are not always the noisiest and the most spectacular. God does not always speak in the sound of the wind and the fire and the earthquake. His word is sometimes heard in the still small voice.

That which is destructive is generally noisy. The loudest politician is not always the most able statesman. The clamoring voice of the majority is no guarantee of the truth and value of that which they acclaim.

The quiet Christian who lives a life of daily obedience to God is worth more to the world than all its noisy demagogues.

> O Sabbath rest by Galilee!
>   O calm of hills above,
> Where Jesus knelt to share with thee
> The silence of eternity,
>   Interpreted by love!
>
> Drop thy still dews of quietness
>   Till all our strivings cease;
> Take from our souls the strain and stress,
> And let our ordered lives confess
>   The beauty of thy peace.

Breathe through the heats of our desire
 Thy coolness and thy balm;
Let sense be dumb, let flesh retire:
Speak through the earthquake, wind and fire,
 O still small voice of calm.
      —*John G. Whittier*

*   *   *

AT HIS FEET

How frequently in the Gospels we read of men and women at the feet of Jesus. As He sat at meat one day a woman of the street came and kissed His feet, washing them with her tears and drying them with her hair (Luke 7:38). Coming with tears of remorse for her sins, she found forgiveness at His feet. So does any sinner.

Christ cast a legion of demons out of a poor creature living naked in the tombs (Luke 8:27-35), and when he was next seen by those who knew him, he was clothed, "sitting at the feet of Jesus." Here at His feet no demon can control and here the one who has experienced His miraculous power in his life should desire to remain, looking up into His face.

On another occasion a ruler of the synagogue ran to Jesus and flung himself at His feet, begging Him to come to His house where his little daughter, twelve years old, lay dying (Luke 8:41, 42). Here was a man bringing his need to the feet of Christ. Here we may, too, make our desires known; here we can plead our needs with the assurance of having them heard and satisfied.

A leper that Christ had cleansed came back to fall in thanksgiving at His feet (Luke 17:16). This is the position to which gratitude should force us who know His mercy and His love. When we have seen His goodness, how can we fail to kneel in praise at His feet!

John on the isle of Patmos beheld Christ in glory and fell at His feet as dead (Revelation 1:17). No man can behold

the glory of the Son of God without being conscious of
his own humility and unworthiness and weakness.

There is a day coming when all things shall be put under
His feet. Every knee shall bow to Him. Kings will cast
their crowns before Him. Then those who have loved Him
here will have the joy of reigning with Him in glory. Now
we may in the study of His Word and in communion with
Him sit at His feet to be taught by Him.

> Master, no offering
> Costly and sweet,
> May we, like Magdalene,
> Lay at Thy feet;
> Yet may love's incense rise,
> Sweeter than sacrifice,
> Dear Lord, to Thee.
>
> Daily our lives would show
> Weakness made strong,
> Toilsome and gloomy ways
> Brightened with song;
> Some deeds of kindness done,
> Some souls by patience won,
> Dear Lord, to Thee.
>
> Some word of hope for hearts
> Burdened with fears,
> Some balm of peace for eyes
> Blinded with tears,
> Some dews of mercy shed,
> Some wayward footsteps led,
> Dear Lord, to Thee.
>
> Thus, in Thy service, Lord,
> Till eventide
> Closes the day of life,
> May we abide;
> And when earth's labors cease,
> Bid us depart in peace,
> Dear Lord, to Thee.
>
> *—Edwin P. Parker*

* * *

"What Shall I Render Unto the Lord?"
Psalm 116:12

FATHER KNOWS BEST

IT IS a good thing that God does not always answer our prayers in just the way in which we take for granted that He will. Sometimes we expect Him to say, "Yes," but instead He says, "No."

We are often like children who are conscious only of the fact that we want something, and because we want it we ask God for it. If a little son should ask his father for a knife, of course, a wise and loving father would not give it to him since he might be injured by it. God, who is not only infinite in His love but who is also infinitely wise, knows that the thing we sometimes desire would not be for our good. In His mercy He refuses us that which, while desirable from our standpoint, He knows would be harmful. We know the immediate desire; God sees the eternal result.

Elijah, discouraged, thought he was the only one left alive who loved and honored God, and he prayed to die. Instead of sending death to the prophet, the Lord made him know that there were seven thousand faithful servants of God left, and Elijah's petition was never granted then or later, for he *never* died. Instead, he was taken into heaven by a whirlwind and a chariot of fire. Elijah, under the juniper tree, was ready to give up the struggle, but God had further work for him to do. Elijah, depressed and discouraged, made an unwise request. God, who saw rich ministry stretching out ahead, who planned to send a heavenly chariot to take the prophet home when that work was completed, would have been unkind had He answered Elijah's prayer by granting him his request for death.

The trouble with Elijah's prayer was this: it was not in the will of God. We should be sure that our prayers are always in line with His will. Christ Himself set us the example when He prayed, "O my Father, if it be possible, let this cup pass from me: nevertheless not as I will, but as thou wilt" (Matthew 26:39).

Father, I know that all my life
 Is portioned out for me;
The changes that are sure to come
 I do not fear to see;
I ask Thee for a present mind
 Intent on pleasing Thee.

I ask Thee for a thoughtful love,
 Through constant watching wise,
To meet the glad with joyful smiles,
 And wipe the weeping eyes;
A heart at leisure from itself,
 To soothe and sympathize.

I ask Thee for the daily strength,
 To none that asked denied,
A mind to blend with outward life
 While keeping at Thy side;
Content to fill a little space,
 If Thou be glorified.

And if some things I do not ask
 Among my blessings be,
I'd have my spirit filled the more
 With grateful love to Thee;
More careful, not to serve Thee much,
 But please Thee perfectly.

In service which Thy love appoints
 There are no bonds for me;
My secret heart is taught the truth
 That makes Thy children free:
A life of self-renouncing love
 Is one of liberty.

—Anna L. Waring

* * *

IN "MITE-Y" MEASURE

STANDING one day in the Temple, the Lord Jesus Christ watched the crowd pass by and cast their offerings into the treasury. Rich men passed by casting in large gifts. Then came a poor widow who dropped in two mites, about a quarter of a cent in our money. The Saviour called His disciples unto Him and said to them, "Verily I say unto you, That this poor widow hath cast more in, than all they which have cast into the treasury: for all they did cast in of their abundance; but she of her want did cast in all that she had, even all her living" (Mark 12:43, 44). A gift is to be judged not by its value but by the spirit in which it is given. An offering is to be measured not by the amount given but by the amount left after the gift has been offered. In the Temple that day, rich men brought rich gifts. Doubtless some gave because their social position demanded it. Some gave out of compliance with tradition. Possibly some gave to be seen of men and admired for their beneficence. Some may have given out of a natural generosity of heart. But all of them had infinitely more left over for themselves than they gave to the Lord. A poor widow, who must have made her offering out of a heart full of love for God, since her circumstances were such that no one could have expected her to give, nevertheless cast in her offering. Having given, she retained nothing. Her gift was greatest because she alone of all who made offerings that day did not consider herself.

It is fine to give generously to the Lord's work. Sometimes, however, our gifts come not from hearts full of love but from either a cold sense of obligation or from fear of what people will think of us if we do not give. Judged by the standard which Christ fixed that day in the Temple, most of us give poor gifts because we keep much more than we give away.

God wants our gifts, but He wants more than the gifts. He wants the giver. Our money is not enough. God wants

our hearts. The truly surrendered child of God considers
all that he has—possessions, family, life itself—not his but
God's. He has given to God everything that he possesses.
The gift is given and the giver also.

> Lord, in the strength of grace,
>   With a glad heart and free,
> Myself, my residue of days,
>   I consecrate to Thee.
>
> Thy ransomed servant, I
>   Restore to Thee Thine own;
> And, from this moment, live or die
>   To serve my God alone.
>   —*Charles Wesley*

*   *   *

A PIECE OF ROPE

WICKED men were waiting at the gates of Damascus to
kill the Apostle Paul. Since it was impossible for him to
get out of the city by means of the gates without falling into
the hands of these men, friends let Paul over the wall in
a basket.

A man's life depended upon a piece of rope and a wicker
basket. These were little, inexpensive things, but very important in that situation. They sustained more than the
physical weight of the man. On that rope depended the
future ministry of Paul to Israel and his preaching to
the Gentiles. On that piece of cord hung suspended the
blessing which was to come into thousands of lives through
Paul's work and words. In that basket were all the churches
Paul was to found in Asia Minor and in Greece. In that
basket were all the converts Paul was to make throughout
the ancient world, and all the epistles which he was yet to
write—full of instruction and blessing to every generation
that has opened the Word of God and read them.

Little things — a life preserver for a drowning man, a glass of water for the desert traveler faint with thirst, a crust of bread for one dying of starvation—are tremendous things! A train may be wrecked because of a small flaw in the steel of the rail or because one spike has become loosened from the crosstie; one match can start a fire which destroys a city. Trifles can change the course of history. A few words can ruin a reputation. One act can wreck a life.

A great universe is made up of atoms and electrons. The God who is the God of the universe is also the God of little things. The God who used the rod of Moses to bring plagues on Egypt and who took five loaves and two fishes from the lunch basket as a little boy and fed thousands can use our little talents and these poor lives. Upon one word of ours may hang the eternal destiny of some soul. Upon some thoughtless act may hinge the course of a life.

If we surrender to God all we possess, however weak and unimportant and useless it may seem to us, He will bless and use it beyond our expectation and in excess of all we can imagine.

> What will it matter in a little while
> That for a day we met and gave a word,
> A touch, a smile upon the way?
> What will it matter whether hearts were brave
> And lives were true, that you gave me
> The sympathy I craved, as I gave you?
>
> These trifles, can it be
> They make or mar a human life?
> Are souls as lightly waved as rushes
> Are by storm or strife? Yeah! Yeah!
>
> A look the failing heart may break,
> Or make it whole.
> And just a word said for love's sweet sake
> May save a soul.
>
> —*Anonymous*

* * *

PRESUMPTUOUS ARGUMENTS

IT IS strange how men will argue with God. He spoke to Moses from the burning bush, telling him He had chosen him to lead Israel out of the Egyptian bondage. One would expect that Moses would have been willing to trust the Lord's judgment to choose the right man for the job. Was he? If you will turn to chapters 3 and 4 of Exodus you will find the answer. Those two chapters are filled with the arguments of Moses used in an effort to convince God that He had made a mistake.

Gideon was guilty of the same attitude. God sent an angel to him with a divine commission to free the people of Israel from the oppression of the Midianites. Instead of being humbly grateful that God had chosen him for such a task and going forth with confidence to accomplish the work which God had selected him to perform, he was full of mealy-mouthed protestations that his family was "poor in Manasseh," and that he was "the least in [his] father's house" (Judges 6:15).

Look at Jeremiah. Courageous soul and uncompromising in his loyalty to the Lord in the face of persecution and oppression though he was, he, too, when he first heard the voice of God calling him for the special service argued that he was not the right man. "I am a child" (Jeremiah 1:6), he said. What he meant was, "I am not big enough for the job. You had better choose somebody else."

How greatly God used these three men! What triumphant plans He had in mind for each, and how fully those plans were realized, but first He had to overcome their objections as each said in effect when He called him, "I am not the right man. You had better get somebody else." God knows the need, and He always chooses the right man to meet the need. God is not so much interested in great talent and ability as He is in simple obedience. He will provide the skill and the power. He asks the man or the woman whom He selects and calls to provide a yielded heart and a surrendered will.

> Time was, I shrank from what was right
> From fear of what was wrong;
> I would not brave the sacred fight,
> Because the foe was strong.
>
> But now I cast that finer sense
> And sorer shame aside;
> Such dread of sin was indolence,
> Such aim at heaven was pride.
>
> So when my Saviour calls, I rise
> And calmly do my best;
> Leaving to Him, with silent eyes
> Of hope and fear, the rest.
>
> I step, I mount where He has led;
> Men count my haltings o'er;
> I know them; yet though self I dread,
> I love His precept more.
>
> —*John Henry Newman*

* * *

"CHOOSE YE THIS DAY"

"God is on our side," said the counselor to the statesman. "I am not eager to have God on my side," he replied. "My concern is to be sure that I am on God's side."

The man who takes his place on the side of the almighty God is the man who chooses victory and immortality. "He that doeth the will of God abideth for ever" (I John 2:17). God's plan shall be perfected. God's will shall be performed. "The battle is the Lord's" (I Samuel 17:47). The triumph shall be His and the man who puts himself on the side of the Conqueror will share in the glory of the conquest.

The man who does God's will has at his command all the omnipotence of Deity. Charles Haddon Spurgeon, the great preacher, declared, "Luther's strength lay in the way in which he laid the burden of the Reformation on the Lord. Continually in prayer he pleaded, 'Lord, this is Thy cause, not mine. Therefore, do Thy own work: for if this Gospel does not prosper, it will not be Luther alone who will be a loser, but Thine own Name will be dishonored.' "

Queen Elizabeth once said to a merchant whom she sent abroad in her service and who was worried about what would happen to his business in his absence, "You mind my business and I will mind yours." The man who is busy about God's business most successfully takes care of his own.

The life that is successful is the life that joins itself to the program of God. Our prayer should not be for God to go with us, but rather for grace to go with Him. Enoch did not choose a path and invite God to join him. Enoch sought out the direction in which God was going and joined himself to Deity. Enoch walked with God. It is not the business of the servant to plan the journey. It is not the business of the soldier to order the campaign. It is the servant's task to follow the master and the duty of the soldier to obey the orders given him by his commander. The successful life is the life planned and directed by God.

> In the still air the music lies unheard;
> In the rough marble beauty hides unseen;
> To make the music and the beauty needs
> The Master's touch, the Sculptor's chisel keen.

> Great Master, touch us with Thy skillful hand;
> Let not the music that is in us die!
> Great Sculptor, hew and polish us; nor let,
> Hidden and lost, Thy form within us lie!

> Spare not the stroke. Do with us as Thou wilt.
> Let there be naught unfinished, broken, marred.
> Complete Thy purpose, that we may become
> Thy perfect image, Thou our God and Lord.
> —*Horatius Bonar*

*   *   *

HANDS OFF!

SOLOMON, the wisest of men, nowhere demonstrated his wisdom better than in the blessing which he bestowed upon Israel after the dedication of the Temple, which he had built. He said to Israel, "And let these my words, wherewith I have made supplication before the Lord, be nigh unto the Lord our God day and night, that he maintain the cause of his servant, and the cause of his people Israel at all times, *as the matter shall require*" (I Kings 8:59).

Solomon demonstrated his wisdom in not trying to dictate a method to the Lord as to how He should maintain the cause of His people. He was wise enough to realize that as the matter should require the Lord would know how to deal with it.

How much happier men would be if they would commit their lives to God, completely trusting Him to do in His own way the thing which is best. A man who seeks to run his own life, leaving God out and trying to have his own way, will sooner or later find himself in trouble. Some people realize this and seek God's protection and guidance. They go so far as to ask that God's will may be done in their lives, but they then make the mistake of trying to tell God how He should accomplish His purpose and of deciding for Him what method is best. God's judgment needs no help from us. He knows that the method which will solve today's problems will be inadequate for the problems which tomorrow brings. He knows that those things which seem good to us today may prove a curse tomorrow. He knows that those things which we find attractive now we may turn from with repugnance later. He knows that what seems a sure way to victory now may prove a trap to defeat next year.

The wise man commits his life to God and leaves it in the care of His love and divine wisdom, assured that the Lord will maintain his cause "as the matter shall require."

O Lord, fulfill Thy will,
Be the days few or many, good or ill:
Prolong them, to suffice
For offering up ourselves Thy sacrifice;
Shorten them if Thou wilt,
To make in righteousness an end of guilt.
Yea, they will not be long
To souls who learn to sing a patient song:
Yea, short they will not be
To souls on tiptoe to flee home to Thee.
O Lord, fulfill Thy will,
Make Thy will ours, and keep us patient still,
Be the days few or many, good or ill.

—*Christina G. Rossetti*

* * *

THE PRAISE OF WRATH

THERE is no such thing as "blind chance" in the life of God's surrendered children. If there was ever a man who seemed "a victim of circumstances," that man was Joseph. Betrayed by his brothers, sold into slavery, unjustly imprisoned, he had from the standpoint of the world every reason to complain of "hard luck" and "tough breaks." Yet nowhere in the record of his life does the Bible mention that he felt discouraged and dissatisfied. Always he was upheld by the assurance that God directed his life and led his steps. Finally, when the hour came that as the prime minister of Egypt he revealed his identity to the brothers who had sold him into slavery, he said to them, "So now it was not you that sent me hither, but God" (Genesis 45:8). Joseph looked upon the unkindness and hostility of his brothers not as misfortune and hardship that came into his life, but rather as God's means of bringing him to Egypt, that there as God's instrument he might preserve many lives through his administration and wisdom in the day of famine. With this point of view there was no place for bitterness toward his brethren, no desire to "get even," only a kindness of heart and a forgiveness of spirit.

Such faith in the leadership and direction of a sovereign God in our lives should characterize all of us today who love the Lord and believe His Word, and with such faith in God's wisdom, love, and guidance there is no place for worry or unhappiness when the circumstances are not those which we would have chosen, and no place for bitterness against those who wrong or abuse us. All the apparent hardships in Joseph's life worked together for God's purpose and Joseph's good. Joseph committed his way unto the Lord and trusted in Him, and God directed his path. We have the promise that He will do the same for us (Psalm 37:5). The hatred of Joseph's brethren started him on the path to a throne. God turned the evil which they did Joseph into a blessing. A sovereign Lord still makes "all things work together for good to them that love God" (Romans 8:28). In our lives He can make the wrath of men to praise Him (Psalm 76:10) just as surely as He made the wrath of Joseph's brethren abound to His own glory in the life and testimony of that remarkable man.

> Clouds, then the glory of sunset;
> Darkness, then burst of the morn;
> Dearth, then the gentle shower;
> Sacrifice—Truth is born!
>
> The earth-throe, then comes the harvest;
> Silence, and then the word;
> Mist, before the full starlight;
> Discord, ere music is heard!
>
> Erring, and then the forgiveness;
> Heart's-ease, after the strife;
> Passion, and then the refining—
> Death, then the wonder of life!
>
> *—Henry Meade Bland*

*   *   *

FORWARD MARCH

IT IS to be doubted if any group of people were ever more "on the spot" than were the Israelites on the occasion described in the fourteenth chapter of Exodus. As the Lord had promised, they had been led by Moses out of Egypt and were camped upon the shores of the Red Sea. Pharaoh's army had followed them to slay them or bring them back. It looked as if there was no escape. They were between Pharaoh and the Red Sea.

Moses, the leader, was a man of great faith. He knew the Lord had not freed the Israelites from the bondage of Egypt to let them fall victims of the Egyptian army on the beach. "Stand still, and see the salvation of the Lord," he said to the trembling, frightened multitude, adding, "The Lord shall fight for you."

The Lord did fight for them, but not while they "stood still." God said to Moses, "Speak unto the children of Israel, that they *go forward,*" and Moses, following the instruction of God, lifted up his rod over the waters of the sea, and they divided and the children of Israel went through on dry ground. When they were safely across, Moses again lifted up his rod, and the water rushed in to engulf the pursuing Egyptians. The Lord fought for Israel, but the battlefield was in the midst of the divided sea through which they had passed — not where they had encamped and where Moses had instructed them to stand still.

It is a great comfort and a strong source of confidence to know that the Lord will undertake and fight for His own— that the place of our seeming defeat is the place where He can best show His power. But God does not want us to stand still. His command to His children in this day is, in the face of seeming impossibilities, to trust and *move forward.* Of course, there are moments when we have to stand still a little while and wait on the Lord, but when the Lord wants a man in a certain place to do a certain job, He will open the way, even if it takes a miracle as great as the dividing of the Red Sea. God wanted Israel in the Land of Promise. He was to show them His salvation many times there, and on the way there, but He did not intend for them merely to stand still by the Red Sea, and when He said, "Go forward," He made the going possible.

> Lord, carry me.—"Nay, but I grant thee strength
> To walk and work thy way to heaven at length."
>
> Lord, why then am I weak?—"Because I give
> Power to the weak, and bid the dying live."
>
> Lord, I am tired.—"He hath not much desired
> The goal, who at the starting-point is tired."
>
> Lord, dost Thou know? — "I know what is in man;
> What the flesh can, and what the spirit can."
>
> Lord, dost Thou care?—"Yes, for thy gain or loss
> So much I cared, it brought me to the cross."
>
> Lord, I believe; help Thou mine unbelief.
> "Good is the word; but rise, for life is brief.
> The follower is not greater than the Chief:
> Follow thou Me along My way of grief."
> —*Christina G. Rossetti*

* * *

HIDDEN THINGS OF TOMORROW

I AM glad that as a child of God I do not have to plan my own future. I am quite content to leave it in the hand of Him who knows the end from the beginning. That which looks very wise to me today may, in the light of tomorrow's now unborn moments, prove to have been foolish in the extreme. The man who trusts God completely and who accepts with unquestioning obedience the will and commands of God will always find that those things which happen to him today, though they may seem today unfortunate, will tomorrow be golden links in a chain of blessing. Illness, which may necessitate a move to another climate and which seems from the viewpoint of the moment almost a tragedy, may be God's way of putting His child in the place where special blessing awaits him. The bitter waters of sorrow forced to my lips may cause me to cry out for relief to God and in new reliance upon Him I shall find crystal streams of abundant joy.

No man knows what tomorrow will bring forth. The Christian does not need to know, for whatever it brings forth will prove a blessing for him. "All things work together for good to them that love God, to them who are the called according to his purpose" (Romans 8:28). The darkness of sorrow brings to the ear of the Christian the melody of songs which were drowned by the laughter of the day, and the flames of a martyr's death become the wings of a fiery chariot bearing a victorious saint to glory. How wise to leave our tomorrows with Him who orders all our ways!

> I have nothing to do with tomorrow,
> My Saviour will make that His care;
> Its grace and its strength I can't borrow,
> So why should I borrow its care?

* * *

> Jesus, Fountain of my days,
> Well-spring of my heart's delight,
> Brightness of my morning rays,
> Solace of my hours of night!
> When I see Thee I arise
> To the hope of cloudless skies.
>
> Lord, Thy presence on the deep
> Calms the pulses of the sea,
> And the waters sink to sleep
> In the rest of seeing Thee,
> And my oft rebellious will
> Hears the mandate, "Peace, be still!"

Now Thy will and mine are one,
Heart in heart and hand in hand;
All the clouds have touched the sun,
All the ships have reached the land;
For Thy love has said to me,
"No more night!" and "No more sea!"

—George Matheson

*   *   *

SHOES TO FIT

To understand the Bible properly one needs some knowledge of the geography of Bible lands. Without it some verses can mean little to the reader. For example, in Deuteronomy 33, Moses in blessing the tribes of Israel says of Asher, "Let him dip his foot in oil. Thy shoes shall be iron and brass" (Deuteronomy 33:24, 25). The significance of this prophetic blessing is realized when we know something of the territory which Asher received when the tribes of Israel came into possession of the Promised Land. Asher's territory combined fertile land near the base of Mt. Lebanon and rocky hills along the coastline. The fertile country was rich in olive groves and the people trampled barefoot upon the olives in the vats to press out the oil. In the rocky hills they needed shoes reinforced with iron and brass. Ordinary leather shoes would not last long against the sharp stones of the rocky mountain passes. Knowing the topography of the land which Asher came to possess, we understood the meaning of the words of Moses' prophetic blessing upon Asher.

God's children may encourage their hearts with the spiritual significance in these words: "Thy shoes shall be iron and brass." It is this: God provides abundantly for that which we must meet. He knows when we shall have to walk rough mountain trails along the road of life. He will not send us there unshod. God knows when sorrow will come. He will prepare us in advance to endure the sorrow. God knows the temptation which lies in wait. He will "not suffer you to be tempted above that ye are able; but will with the temptation also make a way to escape" (I Corinthians 10:13). The last clause of the verse we should take with the first, "Thy shoes shall be iron and brass; and *as thy days, so shall thy strength be.*"

> Years ago, when I
>   Was jest a little lad,
> An' after school hours used to work
>   Around the farm with Dad,
> I used to be so wearied out
>   When eventide was come,
> That I got kinder anxious-like
>   About the journey home;
> But Dad, he used to lead the way,
> An' once in awhile turn 'round an' say,
>   So cheerin' like, so tender, "Come!
> Come on, my son, you're nearly home!"
>   That allers used to help me some;
> An' so I followed Father home.
>
> I'm old an' gray an' feeble now,
>   An trembly at the knee,
> But life seems just the same today
>   As then it seemed to me.
> For while I am still so wearied out
>   When eventide is come,
> An' still git kinder anxious-like
>   About the journey home,
> But still my Father leads the way,
> An' once in awhile I hear Him say,
>   So cheerin' like, so tender, "Come!
> Come on, My son, you're nearly home!"
>   An' same as then, that helps me some,
> And so I'm following Father home.
>   —*John Talman*

*   *   *

THE MARKET PRICE

A few days before His crucifixion, as our Lord was sitting at meat in the house of His friends in Bethany, Mary came with an alabaster box of precious ointment. She broke the box, poured the ointment upon His head and so anointed Him with it that its perfume filled the room. Mark says of the incident, "And there were some that had indignation within themselves, and said, Why was this waste of the ointment made? For it might have been sold for more than three hundred pence" (Mark 14:4, 5).

These people were right about the value of the ointment. It could have been sold in the market for more than three hundred pence. No one can blame them for knowing the market price of ointment. But Jesus Christ Himself showed how wrong they were in thinking it was being wasted. He said, "Let her alone; why trouble ye her? she hath wrought a good work on me" (Mark 14:6).

Nothing is wasted which is given to God. No treasure is so valuable as when it is broken as an offering to Him. "It might have been sold," but one of the sweetest acts in the whole New Testament would have gone unperformed if it had been. I was talking not long ago to a woman about her profession. I said, "I should think you'd enjoy your work. It seems to me that it affords a wonderful opportunity for service." She replied, "I studied for this profession because it was the easiest way I could think of to make a living." A man or a woman should try to make a living, but what a poor reason for choosing a lifework! That is simply a selling of one's talents and abilities.

There are some people who cannot understand why a man should preach the Gospel since it pays so little. Men who love money and who judge success by the size of a man's income are at a loss to understand why a man will go to Africa as a missionary when he could stay home and become a wealthy man. They are like those who said at Bethany that day, "Why was this waste of the ointment made?" No life is wasted which is offered in service to Christ. The only life which is well invested is that which, like the offering of the alabaster box of ointment, is broken for His sake and offered as a tribute of love to Him.

> Five broken loaves beside the sea and thousands fed,
> As Thy hand, Lord, in breaking, blessed the bread.
> Men would the throng in emptiness have sent away
> Whose need was met with broken bread that day.
>
> A broken vase of priceless worth rich fragrance shed
> In ointment poured in worship on Thy head.
> A lovely thing all shattered thus—*What waste,* they thought.
> But Mary's deed of love Thy blessing brought.
>
> A broken form upon the cross and souls set free.
> Thy anguish there has paid the penalty—
> Sin's awful price in riven flesh and pain and blood—
> Redemption's cost, the broken Lamb of God.
>
> Oh, break my life if it must be.
> No longer mine, I give it Thee.
> Oh, break my will; the off'ring take.
> For blessing comes when Thou dost break.
>
>   —*Bob Jones, Jr.*

*   *   *

Printed in the United States of America